THE AIR FRYER COOKBOOK
with Pictures

Quick & Easy Recipes for Absolute Beginners

Emma K. WIlliams

Full Color Edition

Table of
Contents

Breaded Chicken Wings - pp.19

Introduction

When lockdowns started and I began to work from home and help my kids with their online learning, I discovered how incredibly tricky it was to balance work, family, and preparing healthy meals. I was constantly tight on time and running around to meet everyone's needs. It was obvious that the easiest thing I could do was to reheat leftovers, order food, or heat up frozen meals just to save time. But making these kinds of meals completely sacrifices the healthy eating habits that I wanted to promote to my kids. I had heard some mentions of the benefits of air fryers from my clients and was curious to learn about the ways that I could use them to make healthier meals. So, I ordered myself one and I haven't looked back since.

As a mother and nutritionist, I find the correlation between healthy and quick meals to be the best thing for my family. I believe making healthy meals more accessible to busy families is my calling. I help many different clients within my nutrition practice, and we work together on balancing caloric intakes, the macro-nutrients of meals, and making commitments to keeping our bodies active. For a lot of my clients, balancing these things can be a challenge, and what I see more than anything else is the lack of desire to prepare healthy meals due to the assumption that the meals will take too long to prepare or are too complicated/fussy. With the air fryer, that is no longer the case. Healthy, unique, and delicious meals are made much more accessible no matter if you are a mom on the go or a student looking to maintain a healthy diet in the height of finals season. I know for my family, my kids are often craving the same rotations of meals, from chicken nuggets to mozzarella sticks to cookies. While it's nice to have these meals in moderation, I strive to promote healthy eating habits with them and balance the same kinds of macronutrients that I work on with clients. It's my goal as a mother to make sure my kids are healthy and have their daily balance of fruits, vegetables,

protein, healthy fats, and carbs. Before I discovered the wonders of an air fryer, I would restrict the amounts of fast food or deep-fried foods that I allowed my kids to have. I would have them eating things that were healthy and beneficial for them, but they still lacked the flavors that they were craving. Now my kids are able to enjoy the foods that they love with a healthier flare. The air fryer takes away a lot of the stress of cooking meals that balance all of their daily food needs. Cooking these healthy alternatives also saves so much time! Instead of heating up freezer burnt chicken nuggets, I can cube chicken breasts, control the amount of salt added, and add seasonings and sides that promote their

Boom Boom Shrimps - pp.35

Fried Ravioli - pp.45

healthy diets in half the time it takes to preheat the oven and cook the store-bought chicken nuggets. I can't say that I have the same cravings for chicken nuggets as my kids do, but when it only takes me a couple of minutes to make them chicken nuggets, I can dedicate the rest of the time I would have spent cooking to making a more unique meal for myself.

At the height of staying inside and cooking from home, air frying has become one of the best ways to cook meals that are simple and easy. There are so many unique and delicious possibilities when you cook with an air fryer. This cookbook can be your guide from simple meals like chicken nuggets and chocolate chip cookies to intricate meals like Veracruz -

cod and beef bone marrow that all utilize the same appliance. You can make meals with all of your favorite ingredients that promote healthy habits. Air frying doesn't have to be boring and isn't limited to a few repetitive meals. The air fryer is known for the amazing french fries that you can make, but what about having a stuffed roast beef or kale chips? The opportunities with an air fryer are endless, and in a time when we are more reliant on cooking from home, why not take the first steps to healthy and delicious meals all in one basket?

The Air Fryer Cookbook with Pictures is your guide to delicious air fryer meals that go beyond the conventional and will bring incredible recipes into your kitchen. These recipes are quick and easy which will make prep and cleanup times feel like a breeze. Reimagine what is possible in your air fryer and give home chefs the accessibility to high quality recipes without all of the hassles. Removing the fear of a time commitment and unhealthy eating practices will ensure that every meal is delicious and beneficial for your health as well. It is my sincerest hope that you can create healthy and easy meals at home that encourage healthier eating practices without breaking the bank or consuming too much precious time. Let's discuss the ways to use an air fryer, some tips and tricks that I have picked up in creating countless air fryer recipes, and the best and worst foods to use in your air fryer. This will establish your path to becoming an air fryer expert in no time!

Spinach and Bacon Muffins - pp.13

4

Cooking
Guide

How to Use Your Air Fryer

When you first get an air fryer, it may be confusing how to use it properly. The first and most fundamental rule to using an air fryer is that they are not for deep frying. If you want to fry, grill, or bake a meal, the air fryer is the perfect kitchen appliance. Due to the convection quality in air fryers, they are the perfect appliance to use for fast and easy cooking. Using the air fryer instead of deep frying foods will result in fried foods that are enormously healthier, too. Grilling and frying food takes less time and results in meals that will always come out with the right amount of crispiness. Baking treats will take less time and the mess will be cut in half.

Most air fryers have baskets on the inside that hold the different foods or ingredients, and a convection coil and fan that evenly distribute the heat throughout the basket to cook your

meal. Depending on the model of air fryer that you have, it is important to follow the directions or instructions specific to that device to reach the optimal temperature for your meal without compromising the ingredients.

Also, after each use, make sure you are cleaning the air fryer properly to get rid of any harboring bacteria or lingering odors from old food crumbs. Read your air fryer's manual before you begin to use it for specific instructions on how to maintain your air fryer. Generally, you will want to clean out the basket and crumb tray in between each use. Often, these trays can be placed directly in the dishwasher. I suggest that you clean out the interior of your air fryer at least once a week or between every five cooked meals. A lot of residue can get trapped on the sides of your air fryer and find their way into other meals. Your air fryer should also be turned off and unplugged when you are cleaning its interior. Ensure that you aren't using any harsh chemicals when you are cleaning the air fryer. Think of it as cleaning out the inside of a microwave. You want to use a medium-strength brush or towel and clean thoroughly with a gentle soap or cleaner. I personally use a natural baking soda paste or an equivalent store-bought option so as to not risk any chemical reactions occurring inside the air fryer.

7 Amazing Tips & Tricks

1 - The first fundamental tip to using an air fryer is to always have your preferred cooking oil on hand. While there are some exceptions to this rule, I recommend that you use a light olive oil cooking spray. There are many different brands and preferences for cooking oil and having one on hand will be essential for many air fryer meals. Coating the air fryer basket with cooking oil will ensure that the meal doesn't get stuck in the basket.

Beef 'n' Pork Burgers- pp.34

2 - Another tip when using your air fryer is to make the most of the timer on the air fryer. Many of the meals in this cookbook call for flipping the food halfway through. Utilizing the timer will allow you to set the time for half of the allotted cook time to ensure that you are flipping the food at the right time.

3 - It is important to note that when you are cooking a meal in the air fryer that calls for a sauce or wet dredge, to place a piece of parchment or foil in the air fryer. Without the barrier of the parchment, the sauce will leak through the basket and potentially compromise the integrity of your air fryer.

4 - While foil and parchment are always great to have on hand, it is also important to have other cooking equipment on hand when using an air fryer. Silicone muffin or cupcake molds will make baking cookies and egg muffins that much easier. There are many different types of cooking equipment that would be a perfect pair to the air fryer; silicone cupcake molds and cannoli tubes are two that will be used in this cookbook.

5 - Be sure to place your air fryer in a well-ventilated area. Placing the air fryer against a wall or in a corner can cause a fire hazard in the kitchen. Pull the air fryer away from the wall and allow the ventilation that escapes from the device on all sides to have enough space to ensure your safety. Additionally, be sure to unplug your air fryer in between uses to avoid short-circuiting it.

6 - Many of the recipes that you will find in this cookbook may require multiple batches. The air fryer works by circulating air through the basket to fry the foods, and if you layer or overcrowd the air fryer basket, the food will not be able to cook through properly. Be sure to use the other tips listed and avoid overcrowding your air fryer so that you get a great, evenly-cooked meal every time!

7 - The last trick when cooking with an air fryer is to keep an internal temperature reader on hand. While these recipes do not require you to use one, it can be helpful to check the internal temperature of any ingredients that you are cooking in the air fryer to ensure that they have cooked all the way through. Here are some of the most common foods that you will see in the air fryer recipes and the internal temperature that they need to reach in the center:

COMMON AIR FRYER FOODS	INTERNAL TEMPERATURE
Chicken	165 °F
Turkey	165 °F
Beef	145 °F
Pork	145 °F
Bacon	150 °F
Fish	145 °F
Eggs	145 °F
Duck	165 °F
Beans	135 °F
Rice and Pasta	135 °F
Shellfish	145 °F
Tofu	165 °F
Mushrooms	165 °F
Root Vegetables	205 °F
Leafy Greens	40°F
Peppers and Tomatoes	165 °F
Squash and Cucumbers	165 °F
Fruits	135 °F
Bread and Pastries	210 °F
Dairy	145 °F
Fritters	210 °F
Muffins	200 °F
Donuts	195 °F
Cookies	180 °F

BEST & WORST
AIR FRYER FOODS

The air fryer is an incredibly versatile cooking appliance. I recommend purchasing an air fryer for yourself for the health benefits, the ease of cooking, and the unique dishes you can create. But what foods are the best and worst for the air fryer?

Some foods to try in the air fryer that will have excellent results every time are:

Chicken- The ventilation of the air fryer will ensure that the chicken is always cooked through and juicy.

Fish- A simple solution to cooking flakey fish or fish steaks is the air fryer. You'll be able to have juicy and flavorful fish that is cooked through each time.

Steak- If you are looking to control each recipe you make to get the perfect steak every time, the air fryer will help you do this. With an internal temperature reader and the correct cooking time, you can make the perfect steak from rare to medium-rare to well-done.

Bacon- Many of the recipes in this cookbook will call for bacon, and the air fryer is perfectly capable of delivering perfectly crispy bacon every time! Remember to always place a piece of foil in the basket so that the bacon grease does not leak through the holes in the basket and you'll be golden.

Frozen foods- The air fryer minimizes the effect that the condensation from frozen foods has on the ingredients. Instead of soggy food, the air fryer will crisp up all of your frozen meals.

Starchy vegetables- Potatoes, pumpkins, zucchini, and asparagus will all have a delicious bite to them when you use the air fryer. It's great to have an internal temperature reader for starchy vegetables to make sure they are not over-or under-cooked.

Also, after each use, make sure you are cleaning the air fryer properly to get rid of any harboring bacteria or lingering odors from old food crumbs. Read your air fryer's manual before you begin to use it for specific instructions on how to maintain your air fryer. Generally, you will want to clean out the basket and crumb tray in between each use. I suggest that you clean out the interior of your air fryer at least once a week or between every five cooked meals. A lot of residue can get trapped on the sides of

Cookies- If you like crunchy or chewy cookies, the air fryer will always deliver fast and delicious cookies. Be sure to place a piece of parchment in the basket and you'll get perfect cookies in every batch.

meal. Depending on the model of air fryer that you have, it is important to follow the directions or instructions specific to that device to reach the optimal temperature for your meal without compromising the ingredients.

There are certain foods not to use in the air fryer. The following foods have a much higher likelihood of compromising the integrity of your air fryer or completely dissolving in the air fryer. The worst foods to use are:

Fish- A simple solution to cooking flakey fish or fish steaks is the air fryer. You'll be able to have juicy and flavorful fish that is cooked through each time.

Pasta- There is no safe way to boil water in the air fryer, so attempting to place pasta in the air fryer will not work. However, it is possible to crisp up already cooked pasta.

Rice- The same rules for pasta apply to rice. You need to cook the rice in boiling water and the air fryer doesn't support boiling liquids. However, some of the recipes in this book call for already cooked rice, but just be sure to do this on the stovetop or in a rice cooker.

Popcorn- The kernels are a nightmare! Cooking popcorn in the air fryer can get popcorn kernels stuck in the air fryer and compromise the appliance. If the kernels fall through the holes in the basket, your air fryer will not be able to cook the popcorn and you could risk breaking the air fryer or starting a kitchen fire.

Dehydrated fruit- The air fryer uses a convection cooking method and placing dehydrated food into the air fryer can cause them to completely disintegrate and make clean-up a headache afterward. However, you can turn fresh fruit into dried fruit with an air fryer (like apples or apricots), which is perfectly safe.

Soups and sauces- The air fryer does not work to boil any sauces or soups. There are also holes in the air fryer basket, so placing too much liquid at all in the air fryer will damage the integrity of the air fryer. However, there are recipes in this cookbook that call for light sauces, so be sure to use parchment or foil to avoid any sauce leaking through the holes in the basket.

Peanut oil- This also goes for thicker olive oils. When using the air fryer, the oil has the chance of smoking, and peanut oil has a high smoke point that can potentially release toxic smoke. There have also been some suggestions linking health risks to peanut oil smoke, so proceed with caution.

Halloumi Cheese Burger - pp.44

Recipes

Avocado Egg Boats

 10 Minutes

 12 Minutes

 2 Servings

Ingredients

- 2 large eggs
- 1 avocado
- 2 slices of bacon
- ¼ cup shredded cheese
- ¼ cup fresh parsley
- Salt, pepper, and paprika to taste

Directions

Cook your bacon in the air fryer at 350 °F for 7 minutes or 10 minutes for thick-cut bacon. Meanwhile, slice the avocado in half, remove the pit, and use a spoon to scoop out a space for the egg. Do not take the skin off of the avocado. Crack each egg into half of the avocado. Chop and sprinkle the bacon, parsley, and cheese on top of the avocado. Add a dash of salt, pepper, and paprika to each side. Place the avocado boats into the air fryer at 400 °F for 12-15 minutes.

Nutritional Facts: Kcal 349; Fat 26g; Protein 23.2g; Carbs 4.7g

Spinach and Bacon Muffins

 10 Minutes

 12–15 Minutes

 8–10 Servings

Ingredients

- 6 large eggs
- ¼ cup chopped spinach
- ¼ cup crumbled bacon
- 2 tbsp heavy cream (of any milk)
- ½ cup shredded cheese
- ¼ cup diced potato
- 2 chopped chives

Directions

Cook the bacon in the air fryer at 350 °F for 7 minutes or 10 minutes for thick-cut bacon. Meanwhile, mix the eggs, spinach, heavy cream, and diced potatoes in a bowl. Pour this mixture into silicone muffin molds. Using silicone muffin molds will hold the liquid contents without spilling. Chop and add the cooked bacon to the molds and top with shredded cheese. Place the molds in the air fryer for 12 minutes at 300 °F and top with chives.

Nutritional Facts: Kcal 104; Fat 7.7g; Protein 7.5g; Carbs 1.25g

Hot Pockets

 5 Minutes

 14 Minutes

 8 Servings

Ingredients

- 1 bag gluten-free crescent rolls
- 8 slices prosciutto
- 8 slices Edam cheese
- 2 tbsp. melted butter
- 2 tsp. sea salt
- 2 tbsp. mayonnaise, optional

Directions

Lay the crescent rolls on a floured work surface and pinch together two triangles to create rectangles for the hot pocket. Then, seal the perforated edges with your fingers. Lay a slice of ham and Edam on one side of the dough. Add a dab of mayonnaise on top of the slices. Cover the slices with the other side of the dough and seal edges with a fork. Brush each hot pocket with melted butter and sprinkle with sea salt. Cook hot pockets in the air fryer at 300 °F for 14 minutes.

Nutritional Facts: Kcal 261; Fat 15.7g; Protein 25.3g; Carbs 3.5g

Cheese and Bacon Potatoes

 20 Minutes

 2-5 Minutes

 8 Servings

Ingredients

- 4 russet potatoes
- ½ cup chopped bacon
- ½ cup shredded cheddar cheese
- 2 tbsp. olive oil
- 2 chopped green onion stems
- Salt and pepper to taste
- Sour cream or ranch dressing, optional

Directions

Rinse the potatoes and poke small holes in the skin with a fork or knife. Microwave the potatoes, covered in a wet paper towel, for 10 minutes, flipping them halfway. Meanwhile, cook your bacon in the air fryer at 350 °F for 7 minutes or 10 minutes for thick-cut bacon. Slice potatoes in half and scoop 2 tbsps from the center. Sprinkle cheese and bacon onto the potato and place in the air fryer at 350 °F for 2 minutes. Top with a drizzle of olive oil, dressing, green onions, and salt and pepper.

Nutritional Facts: Kcal 175; Fat 9.3g; Protein 6.5g; Carbs 12g

French Toast Sticks

 5 Minutes

 8-10 Minutes

 6 Servings

Ingredients

- 6 slices brioche bread
- 2 large eggs
- ⅓ cup heavy cream (of any milk)
- 1 tbsp. melted butter
- 2 tbsp. granulated sugar
- 1 tsp. cinnamon
- ½ tsp. vanilla extract
- ½ tsp. salt
- ¼ cup maple syrup

Directions

Slice brioche into strips. In a shallow bowl, whisk together eggs, heavy cream, butter, and vanilla extract. Separately, mix the dry ingredients: sugar, cinnamon, and salt. Dunk each brioche stick into the wet mixture and then sprinkle the dry mixture onto each side. Set the air fryer to 350 °F and cook the strips for 8-10 minutes or until crisp. Pour the maple syrup into a small bowl for dipping.

Nutritional Facts: Kcal 237; Fat 9g; Protein 5g; Carbs 33g

Egg Cups

Ingredients

 10 Minutes

 15 Minutes

 4 Servings

- 4 large eggs
- 4 slices whole-wheat bread
- 2 tbsp. butter
- ¼ cup chopped bacon or 2 slices
- 2 tbsp chopped parsley
- Salt and pepper to taste

Directions

Cook bacon in the air fryer at 350 °F for 7-10 minutes and chop it into bite-sized pieces. Cut the crusts off the whole wheat bread and spread a layer of butter on each side. Lightly coat silicone egg molds or ramekins with non-stick spray and add the buttered bread. Crack each egg into the bread cups, sprinkle bacon on each, and place it in the air fryer at 400 °F for 14 minutes. Top with parsley, salt, and pepper to taste.

Nutritional Facts: Kcal 199; Fat 12.2g; Protein 10g; Carbs 12.3g

Breakfast Burrito

 15 Minutes

 8 Minutes

 8 Servings

Ingredients

- 1 lb. spicy chorizo
- 6 flour tortillas
- 1–1 ½ diced russet potatoes
- 4 large eggs
- 1 cup shredded cheese
- ¼ cup milk
- 2 tbsp. olive oil
- 1 tsp. each of salt, pepper, and paprika

Directions

Dice the potatoes. Coat them in olive oil, salt, pepper, and paprika. Cook in the air fryer at 400 °F for 8 minutes or until the potatoes are crispy. In a sauté pan, on medium heat, break up the chorizo and sauté until browned. Remove chorizo, leave the grease in the pan, and scramble the eggs and milk. Assemble the potatoes, chorizo, eggs, and cheese onto the tortillas. Secure with a toothpick. Fry the burritos in the air fryer at 400 °F for 7–8 minutes.

Nutritional Facts: Kcal 451; Fat 30g; Protein 21g; Carbs 23g

Scotch Eggs

 10 Minutes

 15 Minutes

 6 Servings

Ingredients

- 6 large eggs, soft-boiled and peeled
- 1 lb. breakfast sausage
- 1 tsp. onion powder
- 1 tsp. garlic powder
- ¼ cup grated parmesan
- 1 tbsp. chopped chives
- 1 tbsp. sriracha
- ½ cup mayonnaise
- 2 tsp. lemon juice

Directions

In a bowl, combine onion powder, garlic powder, parmesan, and chives. Once combined, separate and grind the breakfast sausages by hand and add to the dry ingredients. Make 3-inch patties with the sausage mixture. Pat dry the soft-boiled eggs, lightly coat with flour, and surround the eggs with the breakfast sausage mix. In a 350 °F air fryer, cook the scotch eggs for 15 minutes or until the outside is crispy. In a small bowl, mix the sriracha, mayonnaise, and lemon juice.

Nutritional Facts: Kcal 412; Fat 33g; Protein 21g; Carbs 6g

Glazed Apple Fritters

 5 Minutes

 10 Minutes

 10-12 Servings

Ingredients

- 2 Honeycrisp apples
- ¼ cup sugar
- 1 ½ tsp. cinnamon
- ¼ cup milk, plus 1 tbsp.
- 2 large eggs
- ¼ cup butter
- 2 tsp. baking powder
- 1 ½ cups flour
- 1 cup powdered sugar

Directions

In a mixing bowl, combine sugar, flour, baking powder, and 1 tsp cinnamon. In a separate bowl, combine milk, butter, and eggs. Add to dry ingredients and stir in the apples. Place parchment paper in a 350 °F air fryer. Scoop 2 tablespoon balls of the apple mixture into the air fryer and fry for 10 minutes. For the glaze, mix the powdered sugar, 1 tbsp of milk, and ½ tsp of cinnamon in a bowl. After the fritters cool, coat in the glaze.

Nutritional Facts: Kcal 164; Fat 5.4g; Protein 3.2g; Carbs 26g

Breakfast Frittata

 5 Minutes

 15-20 Minutes

 2 Servings

Ingredients

- 4 eggs
- ½ lb. breakfast sausage
- ½ cup milk
- ½ cup red bell pepper
- ½ cup shredded cheese
- ½ diced red onion
- 1 diced green onion
- 1 pinch cayenne pepper
- Salt, pepper, and paprika to taste

Directions

In a mixing bowl, combine eggs, crumbled breakfast sausage, cheese, milk, bell pepper, red onion, cayenne pepper, salt, pepper, and paprika. In a 360 °F air fryer, spray a cake pan with non-stick spray and pour in the frittata mixture. Cook in the air fryer for 15-20 minutes. Check with a toothpick that the eggs are cooked through. Remove the frittata from the air fryer, top with green onion.

Nutritional Facts: Kcal 316; Fat 21g; Protein 22g; Carbs 9.5g

Churros

 10 Minutes

 20 Minutes

 4 Servings

Ingredients

- ¼ cup butter
- 2 large eggs
- ½ cup milk
- ½ cup flour
- ¼ cup white sugar
- ½ tsp. cinnamon
- 1 tsp. salt

Directions

In a saucepan over medium heat, boil the milk with a pinch of salt. Add the flour and stir until a wet dough forms. Allow the dough to cool for 5 minutes. Combine the eggs into the dough and place into a plastic bag. Cut off the tip of the plastic bag, and in a parchment-lined air fryer, pipe the churro dough into the air fryer. Cook each batch for 10 minutes at 375 °F or until golden. Coat each churro with cinnamon and sugar.

Nutritional Facts: Kcal 257; Fat 14.8g; Protein 5.9g; Carbs 26.4g

Chocolate Banana Bread

 10 Minutes

 25 Minutes

 6 Servings

Ingredients

- 2 mashed bananas
- 1 cup chocolate chips
- 2 tbsp. butter
- 2 large eggs
- 1 cup milk
- 2 cups flour
- ¾ cup sugar
- 1 tsp. vanilla extract
- ½ tsp baking powder and baking soda

Directions

In a bowl, combine the butter and sugar until small peaks form. Next, add the eggs and vanilla to the butter and sugar. Mix in the flour, baking powder, and baking soda. Combine the batter well before adding the bananas and milk. Add the chocolate chips last. Pour into an air fryer-safe pan, coat with cooking spray, and cook at 350 °F for 25 minutes.

Nutritional Facts: Kcal 511; Fat 15.2g; Protein 10.3g; Carbs 84.7g

Breaded Chicken Wings

 10 Minutes

 30 Minutes

 2 Servings

Ingredients

- 1 lb. chicken wings
- 1 whisked egg
- ¼ cup flour
- ¾ cup panko breadcrumbs
- 1 tsp. salt and peppe
- 1 tsp. garlic powder
- 1 tsp. paprika

Directions

In a small bowl, combine salt, pepper, paprika, and garlic powder. Pat dry the chicken wings and dust them with the spice mix. Using three additional bowls, first coat the wings in flour, then in the whisked egg, and last in the panko crumbs. Ensure that each wing is thoroughly coated. In a 350 °F air fryer, cook wings for 15 minutes. Add 5 minutes at 400 °F for extra crunch.

Nutritional Facts: Kcal 533; Fat 17.4g; Protein 70g; Carbs 20g

Chicken Taquitos

 10 Minutes

 15 Minutes

 4 Servings

Ingredients

- 1 shredded rotisserie chicken
- 4 flour tortillas (8-inch)
- ½ cup shredded Mexican blend cheese
- ¼ cup sour cream
- 3 tbsp. Mexican-style salsa
- 1 clove minced garlic
- 2 tbsp. diced onion
- Salt and pepper to taste

Directions

In a skillet, cook onions until translucent. Add the garlic, salsa, cheese, chicken, salt, and pepper to the skillet. sauté the ingredients until the cheese is melted. Spoon about 3 tablespoons of the taquito mix onto the center of the tortillas and roll. Place a half-inch apart in the air fryer at 400 °F and lightly spray with cooking oil. Fry the taquitos for 10 to 15 minutes, flipping halfway.

Nutritional Facts: Kcal 160; Fat 8.4g; Protein 9g; Carbs 12.1g

Asiatic Orange Chicken

 10 Minutes

 15 Minutes

 2 Servings

Ingredients

- 1 lb. cubed chicken breast
- 3 tbsp. cornstarch
- ½ cup orange juice
- 2 tbsp. brown sugar
- 1 tbsp. rice wine vinegar
- 1 tsp. minced garlic
- 1 tsp. minced ginger
- 2 tbsp. soy sauce
- 2 tsp. sesame seeds

Directions

Cube the chicken and lightly coat in the cornstarch. Fry in the air fryer at 400 °F for 10 minutes, shaking the basket halfway to flip the chicken. Meanwhile, in a skillet, combine the orange juice, rice wine vinegar, brown sugar, garlic, ginger, and soy sauce. Simmer for 5 minutes. Add a dash of water and cornstarch to the orange mixture and simmer for another minute. Coat chicken with sauce and sprinkle with sesame seeds.

Nutritional Facts: Kcal 399; Fat 7g; Protein 49g; Carbs 29g

Bacon-Wrapped Chicken Legs

 20 Minutes

 30 Minutes

 2 Servings

Ingredients

- 1 ½ lb. skinless chicken thighs
- 6 slices thick-cut bacon
- ½ stick butter
- ¼ tsp. sage
- ¼ tsp. basil
- 2 tsp. minced garlic
- 1 tbsp. fresh parsley
- Salt and pepper to taste

Directions

In a mixing bowl, combine the softened butter, sage, basil, garlic, salt, and pepper. Allow the mixture to cool. Once cooled, tuck a tsp of the butter mixture into each chicken thigh and wrap with bacon. Secure with toothpicks if needed. Air fry the bacon-wrapped chicken at 375 °F for 25-30 minutes, flipping halfway. Plate the chicken and sprinkle with fresh parsley.

Nutritional Facts: Kcal 663; Fat 57g; Protein 30g; Carbs 1.2g

Chicken Nuggets

 5 Minutes

 15 Minutes

 5 Servings

Ingredients

- ½ lb. chicken breast
- 2 large eggs
- ¼ cup lemon juice
- ¼ cup panko breadcrumbs
- ¼ cup grated parmesan cheese
- 1 tsp. onion powder
- 1 tsp. garlic powder
- 1 tsp. each of salt, pepper, and paprika

Directions

Cube the chicken breasts into bite-size pieces. In a bowl, whisk together the eggs, lemon juice, garlic powder, onion powder, salt, pepper, and paprika. In a separate bowl, combine the panko and parmesan cheese. Dunk the chicken bites into the egg mixture and then thoroughly coat in the panko. Place in the air fryer at 400 °F for 12-15 minutes and lightly spray with cooking oil.

Nutritional Facts: Kcal 133; Fat 4.7g; Protein 16.7g; Carbs 5.3g

Southern Country Sandwich

 10 Minutes

 20 Minutes

 4 Servings

Ingredients

- 1 lb. chicken breast
- 4 burger buns or biscuits
- 1 cup flour
- ½ cup cornstarch
- 1 tbsp. garlic powder
- 2 cups buttermilk
- 2 tsp. each of salt, pepper, and paprika
- Pickles and mayonnaise for topping

Directions

Use two shallow bowls to create the coating for the chicken. In the first bowl, combine the flour, cornstarch, and garlic powder. In the second bowl, combine the buttermilk, salt, pepper, and paprika. Dunk the chicken in the flour mixture, then the buttermilk mixture, then back in the flour. Spray chicken with cooking oil and place in the air fryer at 400 °F for 20 minutes. Flip the chicken halfway and spray again. Assemble on a bun with pickles and mayonnaise.

Nutritional Facts: Kcal 546; Fat 12.7g; Protein 35g; Carbs 70g

Buffalo Wings

 10 Minutes

 20 Minutes

 4 Servings

Ingredients

- 2 lb. chicken wings
- 1 tbsp. olive oil
- ¼ cup hot sauce of choice
- ¼ cup butter
- 1 tsp. garlic powder
- 1 tsp. onion powder
- 1 tsp. Worcestershire sauce
- 1 tsp. salt and pepper

Directions

Pat the chicken wings dry and separate into drums and flats. In a large bowl, coat chicken in olive oil, onion powder, salt, and pepper. Place in the air fryer at 400 °F for up to 20 minutes, checking every 5 minutes for desired crispiness. Meanwhile, in a smaller bowl, combine the hot sauce, butter, garlic powder, and Worcestershire sauce. Remove chicken from the air fryer and generously coat in the buffalo sauce.

Nutritional Facts: Kcal 571; Fat 31g; Protein 66g; Carbs 1.8g

Italian Chicken Piccata

 10 Minutes

 15 Minutes

 4 Servings

Ingredients

- 1 lb. boneless chicken breast
- 2 large eggs
- 2 tbsp. lemon juice
- 1 cup breadcrumbs
- ¼ cup grated parmesan cheese
- ½ cup butter
- 1 cup chicken broth
- ¼ cup capers
- 1 tsp. each of salt, pepper, and garlic powder

Directions

Using a mallet, flatten the chicken breasts until ¼-inch thick. In a shallow bowl, mix the eggs, 1 tbsp of lemon juice, and garlic powder. In another bowl, combine the breadcrumbs and parmesan. Dip chicken breasts into the egg mixture and then the breadcrumb mixture. Spray the air fryer with cooking oil and cook at 350 °F for 15 minutes. Meanwhile, on a medium-heat skillet, whisk together the chicken broth, lemon juice, butter, capers, salt, and pepper. Simmer until the sauce is reduced. Pour over the chicken.

Nutritional Facts: Kcal 586; Fat 36.6g; Protein 42g; Carbs 20g

Duck Breast a l' Orange

 15 Minutes

 20 Minutes

 4 Servings

Ingredients

- 2 lb. boneless duck breast
- 4 large oranges
- ⅓ cup fresh orange juice
- 1 tbsp. butter
- ½ cup minced shallots
- ⅓ cup sugar
- 1 tbsp. flour
- 1 tbsp. parsley
- 1 tsp. each of salt, pepper, and thyme

Directions

Season duck with salt, pepper, thyme, and parsley. Place the duck in the air fryer and surround with shallots. Cut half of the oranges and place on top of the duck. Cook in the air fryer at 360 °F for 15 minutes. Meanwhile, in a medium heat skillet, combine orange juice, butter, sugar, and flour. Slowly add the salt as the sauce begins to caramelize, then add the rest of the orange slices. Top the duck breast with the candied oranges and sauce.

Nutritional Facts: Kcal 498; Fat 12g; Protein 52.5g; Carbs 45g

Whole Chicken

 10 Minutes

 30 Minutes

 4 Servings

Ingredients

- 1 whole chicken
- 2 corn cobs
- 3 diced potatoes
- 3 medium carrots
- 2 medium zucchini or squash
- 2 tbsp. olive oil
- 1 tsp. garlic powder
- 1 tsp. onion powder
- 1 tsp. each of salt, pepper, and paprika

Directions

Rinse and pat dry the chicken. In a small bowl, whisk together olive oil, garlic powder, onion powder, salt, pepper, and paprika. Coat the chicken with the olive oil mixture. Dice and chop the corn, potatoes, carrots, and zucchini and spray with cooking oil. Place the vegetables at the bottom of the air fryer and place the chicken on top. Cook at 360 °F for 30 minutes.

Nutritional Facts: Kcal 291; Fat 11g; Protein 10.7g; Carbs 40g

Pecan Crusted Chicken Breasts

 5 Minutes

 20 Minutes

 2 Servings

Ingredients

- 1 lb. skinless chicken breasts
- 1 cup crushed roasted pecans
- ¼ cup mayonnaise
- 1 tbsp. wholegrain mustard
- ½ cup panko breadcrumbs
- ¼ cup grated parmesan cheese
- 2 whole cucumbers
- Salt and pepper to taste

Directions

Rinse and pat dry the chicken breasts. In a shallow bowl, combine the pecans, breadcrumbs, and parmesan cheese. In a separate bowl, mix the mayonnaise and mustard. Thoroughly coat the chicken breasts in the mayonnaise mixture and then the pecan mixture. Fry the chicken breasts at 360 °F for 20 minutes. While they are cooking, slice your cucumbers into bite-size pieces and coat with salt and pepper.

Nutritional Facts: Kcal 371; Fat 22g; Protein 12g; Carbs 34g

Stuffed Turkey Breast

 15 Minutes

 35 Minutes

 4 Servings

Ingredients

- 2 lb. turkey breast
- ¼ cup bacon or 4 slices
- 2 cups spinach
- ¼ cup feta cheese
- 1 clove minced garlic
- 1 tbsp. breadcrumbs
- 1 large egg
- 2 tbsp. minced onion or shallot
- 1 tsp. each of salt, pepper, thyme, and sage

Directions

a medium-heat saucepan, add 2 tsp of water to e spinach until wilted, add in the onion and garlic til translucent. Cool and squeeze out extra liquid. ook bacon in the air fryer at 350 °F for 7-10 inutes and chop into bite-sized pieces. In a mixing owl, whisk together the bacon, feta, spinach, arlic, onion, breadcrumbs, and egg. Slice turkey reasts in half and pound with a mallet until ½-inch ick. Spread the stuffing on half of the breast and ld the breast in half. Secure with kitchen twine. ace in the air fryer at 360 °F for 20 minutes and en flip for an extra 10-15 minutes.

utritional Facts: Kcal 408; Fat 15g; Protein 50g; arbs 15.7g

Quesadillas

 5 Minutes

 5-7 Minutes

 4 Servings

Ingredients

- 1 lb. pulled rotisserie chicken
- 4 large flour tortillas
- 2 cups Mexican blend cheese
- ⅓ cup mayonnaise
- 2 tsp. hot sauce of choice
- 1 tsp. sugar
- 1 tsp. each of salt, pepper, garlic powder and paprika

Directions

Shred the rotisserie chicken into bite-sized pieces. In a bowl, mix the chicken and cheese. Assemble the quesadilla by placing a layer of chicken and cheese between tortillas. Spray the base of the air fryer with cooking oil and fry at 370 °F for 5 minutes. For extra crispiness, flip and fry for an additional 2 minutes. Meanwhile, in a small bowl, whisk together the mayonnaise, hot sauce, sugar, salt, pepper, garlic powder, and paprika.

Nutritional Facts: Kcal 589; Fat 41.3g; Protein 35g; Carbs 20g

Korean Chicken Wings

 10 Minutes

 20-30 Minutes

 4 Servings

Ingredients

- 2 lb. chicken wings
- ½ cup corn starch
- ⅓ cup kimchi
- ⅓ cup pickled radish
- 3 tbsp. gochujang
- 1 tbsp. brown sugar
- ¼ cup honey
- 2 tsp. minced garlic
- 1 tsp. each of salt, pepper, onion and garlic powder

Directions

In a medium-heat saucepan, whisk together the gochujang, brown sugar, honey, minced garlic, and onion powder. Let the sauce simmer and reduce for 5 minutes. Place the chicken wings, separated into flats and drums, in a large bowl and toss with the corn starch, salt, pepper, and garlic powder. In a 400 °F air fryer, cook wings for 20 minutes. Spray the wings with cooking oil and flip halfway. Leave them in for an extra 5-7 minutes for extra crispiness. Coat the cooked wings in the gochujang sauce and plate with the kimchi and pickled radish.

Nutritional Facts: Kcal 628; Fat 16.8g; Protein 66g; Carbs 48g

Turkey Meatballs

 5 Minutes

 8 Minutes

 6 Servings

Ingredients

- 1 lb. ground turkey
- 1 large egg
- 1 tbsp. dijon mustard
- ⅓ cup breadcrumbs
- ¼ cup parmesan cheese
- 1 tbsp. olive oil
- 1 tsp. garlic powder
- 1 tsp. dried parsley
- Salt and pepper to taste

Directions

In a large mixing bowl, combine the ground turkey, egg, dijon mustard, breadcrumbs, parmesan, olive oil, garlic powder, parsley, salt, and pepper. Roll each meatball into 2-inch balls. Place a piece of parchment in your air fryer and spray the meatballs with cooking oil. Do not overlap meatballs. Fry at 400 °F for 8 minutes.

Nutritional Facts: Kcal 210; Fat 12g; Protein 23g; Carbs 4.9g

Southern Style Tenders

 5 Minutes

 20 Minutes

 4 Servings

Ingredients

- 1 lb. chicken thighs
- ¾ cup buttermilk
- 1 ¼ cup breadcrumbs
- ¼ cup parmesan cheese
- 2 tsp. minced garlic
- 1 tsp. each of salt, pepper, and paprika

Directions

Rinse and pat dry the chicken thighs. In a shallow bowl, mix the buttermilk, garlic, and salt. In an additional shallow bowl, combine the breadcrumbs, parmesan, pepper, and paprika. Marinate the chicken thighs in the buttermilk and coat the thighs in the breadcrumbs. In a 370 °F air fryer, fry the chicken thighs for 15 minutes, flipping halfway. Raise the temperature to 400 °F for another 5 minutes for extra crispness.

Nutritional Facts: Kcal 263; Fat 9.3g; Protein 35.6g; Carbs 7.4g

Roastbeef

 5 Minutes

 40 Minutes

 6 Servings

Ingredients

- 2 lb. roast beef
- 1 medium diced onion
- 2 tsp. rosemary
- 2 tsp. thyme
- 1 tbsp. olive oil
- Salt and pepper to taste

Directions

Rinse and pat the roast dry. In a small bowl, whisk together the olive oil, rosemary, thyme, salt, and pepper. Thoroughly coat the roast in the olive oil mixture. Dice the onion. Place the marinated roast into the air fryer and tuck the diced onion under and on top of the roast. Fry at 400 °F for 15 minutes. Flip the roast and reduce the heat to 325 °F for another 15 minutes.

Nutritional Facts: Kcal 311; Fat 11.9g; Protein 46g; Carbs 2.2g

Quesadillas

 10 Minutes

 10-12 Minutes

 4 Servings

Ingredients

- 1 lb. shredded beef
- 2 cups Mexican cheese blend
- 4 flour tortillas
- ¼ cup diced onion
- ¼ cup diced bell pepper
- 1 tsp. lime juice
- 1 tsp. cumin
- 1 tsp. garlic powder
- 1 tbsp. hot sauce of choice
- Salt and pepper to taste

Directions

In a medium-heat skillet, sauté the onions and peppers. When onions are translucent, add beef and sauté for an additional 3-5 minutes. In a small bowl, mix the beef, vegetables, cheese, lime juice, cumin, garlic powder, salt, and pepper. Lay the tortillas flat and fill the center with the beef and vegetable mix and roll the tortillas into tubes. Fry in the air fryer at 370 °F for 10-12 minutes. Serve with hot sauce.

Nutritional Facts: Kcal 277; Fat 12.4g; Protein 39g; Carbs 13.2g

Portobello Pork Medallions

Ingredients

 15 Minutes

 10 Minutes

 4 Servings

- 1 pork tenderloin
- 12 oz. baby bella mushrooms
- 3 tbsp. flour
- ¼ cup breadcrumbs
- 1 tsp. each of onion and garlic powder, salt, pepper, and paprika
- 1 tbsp. butter
- ½ cup apricot preserve
- 2 tbsp. chicken broth
- 1 tsp. rosemary

Directions

Fill a shallow bowl with flour. In a second bowl, combine the breadcrumbs, garlic powder, onion powder, salt, pepper, and paprika. Thoroughly coat the pork tenderloin in the flour and then the breadcrumbs and place in the air fryer at 375 °F for 10 minutes, flipping halfway. Be sure to coat the air fryer with cooking oil. In a medium-heat skillet, combine the mushrooms, butter, apricot preserve, chicken broth, and rosemary. Stir until the sauce is well combined and the preserves are melted. Serve tenderloin with the sauce.

Nutritional Facts: Kcal 316; Fat 6.6g; Protein 26g; Carbs 40.1g

Stuffed Peppers

Ingredients

 15 Minutes

12-15 Minutes

 4 Servings

- 4 bell peppers
- 1 lb. lean ground beef
- 1 can diced tomatoes
- 1 can corn
- 1 can of black beans
- 2 cups cooked rice
- 1 cup shredded cheese
- 1 tbsp. olive oil
- 1 tsp. each of salt, pepper, garlic powder, and parsley

Directions

In a medium-heat skillet, sauté the ground beef. Add the olive oil, tomatoes, corn, black beans, and rice. Season with salt, pepper, garlic powder, and parsley. sauté for 5-7 minutes. Meanwhile, cut the tops off the bell peppers and clean out any seeds. Pour filling into the bell peppers and place in the air fryer at 360 °F for 10 minutes. Add the cheese to the tops of the peppers and fry for another 2-4 minutes.

Nutritional Facts: Kcal 735; Fat 13.7g; Protein 49g; Carbs 102g

Lamb Chops

 1 Hour and 10 Minutes

 14 Minutes

 4 Servings

Ingredients

- 1 ¼ lb. rack of lamb
- 3 tbsp. olive oil
- 1 tsp. minced garlic
- 2 tbsp. chopped rosemary
- 1 tsp. oregano
- 1 tsp. salt and pepper
- ⅓ cup fresh cranberries

Directions

In a large bowl, marinate the lamb chops in olive oil, garlic, rosemary, oregano, salt, and pepper. Allow the lamb chops to marinate in the refrigerator for 1 hour. Spray the air fryer with cooking spray and line with parchment. Place the marinated lamb chop and half of the cranberries into the air fryer and cook at 380 °F for 14 minutes, flipping halfway. Serve with the remaining cranberries.

Nutritional Facts: Kcal 342; Fat 23.3g; Protein 29g; Carbs 2.7g

Roastbeef Tacos

 1 Hour and 20 Minutes

 14 Minutes

 6 Servings

Ingredients

- 1 lb. flank steak
- 1 cup chopped cilantro
- ⅓ cup olive oil
- ⅓ cup lime juice
- 6 flour tortillas
- 4 tsp. minced garlic
- 1 tsp. each of chili powder, cumin, salt, and pepper
- 1 cup shredded lettuce
- 2 diced tomatoes

Directions

In a large bowl, marinate the flank steak with cilantro, olive oil, lime juice, garlic, chili powder, cumin, salt, and pepper. Let the steak marinate in the refrigerator for 1 hour. Spray the air fryer with cooking oil and place the steak in the air fryer at 400 °F for 14 minutes, flipping halfway. Plate the tacos with the flank steak, shredded lettuce, tomatoes, and lime juice.

Nutritional Facts: Kcal 307; Fat 18.3g; Protein 23g; Carbs 13.4g

Meatloaf

Ingredients

 10 Minutes

 15 Minutes

 4 Servings

- 1 lb. ground beef
- ½ diced green bell pepper
- ½ cup diced white onion
- 1 egg yolk
- ¼ cup breadcrumbs
- 2 tbsp. parmesan cheese
- 1 tsp. Worcestershire sauce
- 1 tbsp. ketchup
- 1 tsp. each of parsley, oregano, garlic powder, salt, and pepper

Directions

In a large bowl, combine beef, bell pepper, onion, egg, breadcrumbs, and parmesan. In a smaller bowl, combine the Worcestershire sauce, ketchup, parsley, oregano, garlic powder, salt, and pepper. Pour half of the mixture into the meatloaf. Shape into a loaf and place on a baking tray or aluminum foil. Cook at 375 °F for 10 minutes, add the rest of the Worcestershire mixture to the top and cook for another 3–5 minutes.

Nutritional Facts: Kcal 311; Fat 11.6g; Protein 40.6g; Carbs 9.2g

Pork Belly Bites

Ingredients

 15 Minutes

 20 Minutes

 6 Servings

- 1 lb. pork belly
- 3 tbsp. olive oil
- 1 tsp. garlic powder
- 1 tbsp. brown sugar
- 1 tsp. salt and pepper

Directions

Rinse and pat dry the pork belly, then chop into 1-inch cubes. If they are fully thawed, place them in the refrigerator for 10 minutes to reform for extra crunchiness. In a large bowl, mix the olive oil, garlic powder, brown sugar, salt, and pepper. Coat the pork belly cubes in the sauce. Place the pork belly in the air fryer at 400 °F for 20 minutes, flipping halfway.

Nutritional Facts: Kcal 417; Fat 27.4g; Protein 35g; Carbs 2g

Ingredients

 20 Minutes

 35 Minutes

 8 Servings

- 1 ½ lb. ground beef
- 8 oz. baby bella mushrooms
- 2 sheets Puff Pastry
- 2 large eggs
- 4 tbsp. breadcrumbs
- 3 tbsp. butter
- 1 tbsp. milk
- 1 chopped red onion
- 1 tsp. each of garlic powder, basil, parsley, salt, and pepper

Directions

In a large bowl, combine the beef, eggs, breadcrumbs, parsley, salt, and milk. In a medium-heat saucepan, sauté the onion, mushrooms, and butter until the onions are translucent. Add the garlic powder, basil, and pepper. On a floured work surface, cut the pastry into squares and layer the mushroom mixture and a ½ cup of the marinated meat onto each square. Fold and secure the corners of the pastry with water and cut slits into the top. Brush the top with the leftover egg and milk mixture and place in the air fryer at 320 °F for 35 minutes.

Nutritional Facts: Kcal 584; Fat 34.7g; Protein 33g; Carbs 33.6g

Mongolian Beef

Ingredients

 20 Minutes

 14 Minutes

 4 Servings

- 1 lb. flank steak
- 2 tbsp. olive oil
- 2 chopped green onions
- 2 chopped white onions
- 1 tsp. cornstarch
- 1 tbsp. minced garlic
- ½ cup soy sauce
- ½ cup brown sugar
- 1 tbsp. grated ginger

Directions

Rinse and pat dry the flank steak and cut into ½-inch cubes. In a large bowl, marinate in olive oil, cornstarch, and soy sauce. Let rest for 15 minutes. Spray the air fryer with cooking oil and fry the flank steak at 400 °F for 14 minutes, flipping halfway. Meanwhile, chop the onions and place in a medium-heat saucepan. Add the minced garlic, brown sugar, and grated ginger and cook until the onions start to become translucent. Serve the flank steak with the sauce.

Nutritional Facts: Kcal 401; Fat 16.6g; Protein 34.6g; Carbs 28.2g

Bacon-Wrapped Sausage

 15 Minutes

 20 Minutes

 8 Servings

Ingredients

- 2 lb. pork sausage
- 8 slices of bacon
- ½ cup melted butter
- 1 cup brown sugar
- 1 tsp. salt and pepper

Directions

In a bowl, whisk together the melted butter, brown sugar, salt, and pepper. Slice each bacon strip in half, brush the butter mixture on each strip, and wrap around each sausage. Secure the bacon with a toothpick if needed. Place in the air fryer at 360 °F for 20 minutes, flipping halfway.

Nutritional Facts: Kcal 659; Fat 51.6g; Protein 29g; Carbs 18.2g

Beef Bone Marrow

 24 Hours

 20 Minutes

 4 Servings

Ingredients

- 4 beef marrow bones
- 1 tbsp. minced garlic
- 1 tbsp. lemon juice
- 1 tbsp. date preserves
- 1 tbsp. sea salt
- 1 tsp. fresh thyme

Directions

Fill a large bowl with water and add 1 tsp of sea salt for every 1 cup of water. Submerge the marrow bones in the water and refrigerate for 24 hours. Replace the water every 4 hours. Drain the bones and pat dry. In a small bowl, mix the minced garlic, lemon juice, date preserves, and half of the fresh thyme. Place on a baking tray or aluminum foil in the air fryer at 450 °F for 20 minutes. The bone marrow should start to leak and become puffy when fully cooked. Serve with the rest of the thyme.

Nutritional Facts: Kcal 151; Fat 7.1g; Protein 19.6g; Carbs 2.3g

Grilled Pork Skewers

 2 Hours

 10 Minutes

 4 Servings

Ingredients

- 1 lb. pork shoulder
- ⅓ cup butter
- 3 cloves garlic
- 2 tbsp. soy sauce
- 2 tbsp. brown sugar
- 1 tbsp. fish sauce
- 2 stalks lemongrass
- 1 tsp. each of chili powder, salt, and pepper

Directions

Rinse and pat dry the pork shoulder. Cube into 1-inch pieces. In a bowl, combine the butter, garlic, soy sauce, brown sugar, fish sauce, lemongrass, chili powder, salt, and pepper. Marinate the pork shoulder cubes in the sauce for 2 hours. Place the pork shoulder cubes onto the skewers and fry in the air fryer at 380 °F for 10 minutes, flipping halfway.

Nutritional Facts: Kcal 497; Fat 39.7g; Protein 28g; Carbs 6.9g

Rib-Eye Steak

 5 Minutes

 15 Minutes

 2 Servings

Ingredients

- 2 lb. rib-eye steak
- ¼ cup olive oil
- ½ cup soy sauce
- 2 tsp. oregano
- 2 tsp. garlic powder
- 2 tsp. salt and pepper

Directions

In a small bowl, whisk together the olive oil, soy sauce, oregano, garlic powder, salt, and pepper. Rinse and pat dry the steak. Brush the marinade onto the rib-eye and place in the air fryer. Cook at 400 °F for 14 minutes, flipping halfway. For a medium steak, cook for an extra minute on each side.

Nutritional Facts: Kcal 579; Fat 50.5g; Protein 25g; Carbs 9.2g

Beef 'n' Pork Burgers

 15 Minutes

 8 Minutes

 3 Servings

Ingredients

- ½ lb. ground beef
- ½ lb. ground pork
- ½ cup flour
- 2 large eggs
- ½ tbsp. butter
- ½ cup breadcrumbs
- 2 tbsp. minced garlic
- 2 tbsp. chopped cabbage
- 1 tsp. salt and pepper

Directions

In a large bowl, combine the ground beef, ground pork, butter, minced garlic, and cabbage. Form 3-inch discs with the meat mixture. Using three shallow bowls, place flour in the first bowl, whisk the eggs in the second bowl, and the third bowl, combine the breadcrumbs, salt, and pepper. Dunk the meat in the flour then the egg and then the breadcrumbs. Fry the tenders at 370 °F for 8 minutes, tossing halfway.

Nutritional Facts: Kcal 473; Fat 13.8g; Protein 52g; Carbs 32g

Pork Chops

 5 Minutes

 20 Minutes

 4 Servings

Ingredients

- 4 boneless pork chops
- 2 tbsp. olive oil
- ½ cup grated parmesan
- 1 tsp. kosher salt
- 1 tsp. paprika
- 1 tsp. garlic powder
- 1 tsp. onion powder
- ½ tsp. ground black pepper

Directions

Pat pork chops dry with paper towels, then coat both sides with oil. In a large bowl, combine spices and grated parmesan. Coat both sides of pork chops with parmesan mixture. Place pork chops in the air fryer basket and cook at 375 °F for 9 minutes, flipping halfway through. Serve and enjoy.

Nutritional Facts: Kcal 337; Fat 24g; Protein 31.3g; Carbs 3.4g

Boom Boom Shrimps

Ingredients

 20 Minutes

 6 Minutes

 4 Servings

- 1 lb. jumbo shrimp
- ¾ cup cornstarch
- ½ cup buttermilk
- 1 cup breadcrumbs
- 1 chopped green onion
- 1 cup mayonnaise
- ½ cup Thai chili sauce
- 2 tbsp. sriracha
- 1 tsp. salt and pepper

Directions

Rinse and peel the shrimp. Using three shallow bowls, place cornstarch in the first bowl, buttermilk in the second bowl, and in the third bowl, combine the breadcrumbs, salt, and pepper. Dunk the shrimp in the flour, then egg, and then breadcrumbs. Spray the air fryer with cooking oil and fry the shrimp at 400 °F for 6 minutes, tossing halfway. Meanwhile, combine the mayonnaise, chili sauce, and sriracha to create the boom boom sauce. Serve with a sprinkle of green onion.

Nutritional Facts: Kcal 561; Fat 21.4g; Protein 26g; Carbs 66.5g

Crab Cakes

Ingredients

 40 Minutes

 15 Minutes

 4 Servings

- 8 oz. lump crab meat
- 1 large egg
- 1 tbsp. mayonnaise
- ½ cup breadcrumbs
- ¼ cup chopped red bell pepper
- 1 chopped green onion
- 1 tbsp. Dijon mustard
- 1 tsp. salt and pepper

Directions

In a large bowl, combine the crab meat, egg, mayonnaise, breadcrumbs, bell pepper, green onion, dijon mustard, salt, and pepper. Refrigerate for 30 minutes. Shape the crab cakes into 3-inch discs that are ½-inch thick. Spray the air fryer with cooking oil and fry the crab cakes at 370 °F for 10 minutes. Flip and fry for an additional 4 minutes for extra crispiness.

Nutritional Facts: Kcal 134; Fat 8g; Protein 12g; Carbs 13g

Bacon-Wrapped Scallops

 10 Minutes

 7 Minutes

 8 Servings

Ingredients

- 1 lb. bay scallops
- ½ lb. bacon or 12 slices
- 2 tbsp. maple syrup
- 1 tsp. olive oil
- 1 tsp. each of salt, pepper, and paprika

Directions

Cook your bacon in the air fryer at 350 °F for 4 minutes or 6 minutes for thick-cut bacon so that it is undercooked. Rinse and pat dry the scallops. In a small bowl, marinate scallops in olive oil, salt, pepper, and paprika. Cut the bacon in half and brush with maple syrup. Wrap bacon around each scallop and secure with a toothpick. Place in the air fryer at 390 °F for 7 minutes or until the bacon looks crispy.

Nutritional Facts: Kcal 443; Fat 25.7g; Protein 40g; Carbs 10.2g

Crusted Salmon

 10 Minutes

 10 Minutes

 2 Servings

Ingredients

- 2 8oz. salmon fillets
- 1 large egg white
- 2 tbsp. butter
- 2 tbsp. olive oil
- ½ cup chopped macadamia nuts
- ½ cup chopped cilantro
- 2 lemons
- 1 tsp. salt and pepper

Directions

Rinse and pat dry the salmon. Coat the salmon in salt and pepper and allow to sit for 5 minutes. Whisk the egg white until frothy and dip the salmon fillets into the egg white. In a small bowl, combine the macadamia nuts, olive oil, and cilantro. Coat the tops of the fillets in the macadamia mixture. Place in a baking dish with butter and the juice of one lemon.Cook in the air fryer at 400 °F for 10 minutes and allow the salmon to soak up the butter. Serve with slices of lemon.

Nutritional Facts: Kcal 763; Fat 63.2g; Protein 46g; Carbs 11g

Salmon Patties

Ingredients

 10 Minutes

 15 Minutes

 4 Servings

- 14 oz. canned salmon
- ¾ cup breadcrumbs
- 1 large egg
- ⅓ cup mayonnaise
- 2 tbsp. lemon juice
- ½ cup diced onion
- 3 tbsp. chopped cilantro
- 1 tsp. each of salt, pepper, and paprika

Directions

In a large bowl, combine the salmon, breadcrumbs, egg, mayonnaise, lemon juice, diced onion, cilantro, salt, pepper, and paprika. Form the salmon mixture into 3-inch patties. Spray the air fryer with cooking oil and cook the salmon patties at 400 °F for 15 minutes, flipping halfway. Use a toothpick to check that the patties are cooked through.

Nutritional Facts: Kcal 313; Fat 15g; Protein 23.9g; Carbs 20.9g

Grilled Tuna Steak

Ingredients

 30 Minutes

 8 Minutes

 4 Servings

- 4 8oz. tuna steaks
- 2 tbsp. lemon juice
- 1 tbsp. olive oil
- 1 tbsp. soy sauce
- 2 tbsp. minced garlic
- 1 chopped green onion
- 1 tsp. each of dried thyme, salt, and pepper

Directions

Rinse and pat dry the tuna steaks. In a large bowl, combine the olive oil, soy sauce, lemon juice, minced garlic, green onion, thyme, salt, and pepper. Allow the tuna steaks to marinate in the sauce for 15-30 minutes. Place the tuna steaks in the air fryer at 380 °F for 8 minutes, flipping halfway.

Nutritional Facts: Kcal 282; Fat 5.6g; Protein 54.1g; Carbs 2.3g

Breaded Fish Sticks

 10 Minutes

 10 Minutes

 4 Servings

Ingredients

- 1 lb. cod fillets
- ½ cup flour
- 1 large egg
- ½ cup breadcrumbs
- ¼ cup parmesan cheese
- 1 tsp. garlic powder
- 1 tsp. each of salt, pepper, and paprika
- 1 lemon

Directions

Rinse, pat dry, and cut the cod into strips. Using three shallow bowls, place flour in the first bowl, whisk eggs in the second bowl, and in the third, combine the breadcrumbs, parmesan, garlic powder, salt, pepper, and paprika. Dunk the cod in the flour, then the egg, then the breadcrumbs. Fry in the air fryer at 400 °F for 10 minutes, tossing halfway. Squeeze lemon juice onto each fish stick.

Nutritional Facts: Kcal 270; Fat 6.2g; Protein 29.8g; Carbs 24.1g

Veracruz Style Tilapia

 10 Minutes

 15 Minutes

 4 Servings

Ingredients

- 4 4oz. tilapia fillets
- 1 ¼ cup diced tomatoes
- 2 diced Yukon gold potatoes
- ¼ cup capers
- ½ cup pitted olives
- 3 tbsp. olive oil
- 3 tbsp. minced garlic
- 4 bay leaves
- 1 tsp. salt, pepper, and chili powder

Directions

In a medium-heat skillet, sauté the tomatoes in olive oil for 5 minutes. When they begin to wilt, add the garlic. In a bowl, combine the sauce, olives, capers, potatoes, bay leaves, salt, pepper, and chili powder. On a baking pan or aluminum foil, pour the sauce onto the tilapia. Cook in the air fryer at 400 °F for 12–15 minutes.

Nutritional Facts: Kcal 294; Fat 13.8g; Protein 24g; Carbs 22.3g

Shrimp Tacos

Ingredients

 18 Minutes

 10 Minutes

 4 Servings

- 1 tbsp. olive oil
- 24 deveined, peeled, and without tail shrimps
- 1 ½ tsp. brown sugar
- ½ cup chopped red onion
- lime wedges
- 12 flour tortillas
- ½ tsp. garlic powder
- ¼ tsp. salt
- 1 cup avocado, sliced
- 1 cup purple cabbage, chopped

Directions

Thaw the shrimp rinsing the frozen shrimp under cold water. Brush the air fryer basket with olive oil. Preheat the air fryer to 400 °F. Stir together the sugar, garlic powder, and salt. Dry the shrimp with paper towels. Place the shrimp in a zippered plastic bag. Pour in the seasoning mixture and shake to coat the shrimp fully. Place the shrimp in the air fryer basket. Cook for 3 - 4 minutes. Turn the shrimp over and cook for 3 - 4 more minutes. Assemble tacos with all the ingrendiets and garnish with your favorite sauce.

Nutritional Facts: Kcal 295; Fat 23g; Protein 22g; Carbs 11g

Land & Sea Cod Fillet

Ingredients

 10 Minutes

 15 Minutes

 2 Servings

- 2 6oz. cod fillets
- ¼ cup butter
- 3 tbsp. olive oil
- 1 lemon
- ½ lb. asparagus
- 6 oz. baby bella mushrooms
- 1 tsp. each of garlic powder, salt, pepper, and paprika

Directions

Rinse and pat dry the cod fillets. Season with salt, pepper, and paprika. Place in the air fryer with a pat of butter and a slice of lemon. Fry in the air fryer at 400 °F for 15 minutes. Meanwhile, in a medium-heat skillet, sauté the asparagus and mushrooms with the olive oil, the rest of the lemon, and garlic powder. Let the cod sit for 5 minutes and serve with the vegetables and sauce.

Nutritional Facts: Kcal 531; Fat 45.5g; Protein 25g; Carbs 12.5g

Salmon and Quinoa Patties

 10 Minutes

 10 Minutes

 4 Servings

Ingredients

- 12 oz. canned salmon
- 1 tsp. olive oil
- 2 large eggs
- ¾ cup cooked quinoa
- ¼ cup mayonnaise
- ½ cup breadcrumbs
- 2 tsp. lemon zest
- ½ tsp. dried dill
- 1 tsp. each of salt, pepper, and paprika

Directions

Drain the salmon and combine, in a large bowl, with the olive oil, eggs, quinoa, mayonnaise, breadcrumbs, lemon zest, dill, salt, pepper, and paprika. Form 3-inch discs about ½-inch thick. Spray the air fryer with cooking spray and fry the salmon patties at 390 °F for 8 minutes. Flip and fry for an additional 2-3 minutes.

Nutritional Facts: Kcal 387; Fat 16.5g; Protein 26.1g; Carbs 34.2g

Shrimp Tostada

 10 Minutes

 6 Minutes

 4 Servings

Ingredients

- 1 lb. jumbo shrimp
- 2 tbsp. lime juice
- 2 sliced avocados
- 1 cup shredded lettuce
- 2 diced tomatoes
- 1 diced red onion
- ¼ cup chopped cilantro
- 4 small flour tortillas
- 1 tsp. each of garlic powder, salt, pepper, and paprika

Directions

Place the flour tortillas in the air fryer at 350 °F for 5 minutes until crispy. Meanwhile, peel and rinse the shrimp. In a large bowl, marinate the shrimp with lime juice, tomatoes, onion, cilantro, garlic powder, salt, pepper, and paprika. Place the shrimp on a baking sheet or aluminum foil in the air fryer at 400 °F for 6 minutes. Assemble the tostadas with shrimp, avocado, and lettuce.

Nutritional Facts: Kcal 370; Fat 20.5g; Protein 25g; Carbs 27.1g

Teriyaki Salmon Skewers

40 Minutes

15 Minutes

2 Servings

Ingredients

- 1 lb. salmon fillets
- 2 tbsp. soy sauce
- 2 tbsp. sesame oil
- 1 tbsp. brown sugar
- 1 tsp. grated ginger
- 1 tbsp. minced garlic
- 2 tsp. sesame seeds
- 1 tsp. salt and pepper

Directions

Rinse, debone, and cut the salmon fillets into 2-inch cubes. In a large bowl, combine the salmon, soy sauce, sesame oil, brown sugar, ginger, garlic, salt, and pepper. Allow the salmon to marinate for 30 minutes. Skewer the salmon cubes and place in the air fryer at 350 °F for 15 minutes. Sprinkle the skewers with sesame seeds.

Nutritional Facts: Kcal 475; Fat 29.2g; Protein 46g; Carbs 9g

Garlic Butter Salmon

10 Minutes

10 Minutes

4 Servings

Ingredients

- 4 6oz. salmon fillets
- 1 tsp minced garlic
- 3 sliced lemons
- 1 tsp. lemon pepper seasoning
- 2 tbsp. olive oil
- 1 tsp. rosemary
- 1 tsp. each of garlic powder, parsley, salt, and pepper

Directions

Rinse and pat dry the salmon. In a bowl, squeeze the juice of one lemon over the salmon and season with minced garlic, lemon pepper, garlic powder, parsley, salt, and pepper. Arrange the salmon on a baking sheet or a piece of aluminum foil and top with sliced lemons and rosemary. Place in the air fryer at 390 °F for 10 minutes.

Nutritional Facts: Kcal 350; Fat 19.2g; Protein 41.7g; Carbs 5.3g

Mahi-Mahi Fillet

 10 Minutes

 15 Minutes

 4 Servings

Ingredients

- 4 6 oz. mahi-mahi fillets
- 4 tbsp. melted butter
- 4 tbsp. parmesan cheese
- 2 cups cooked rice
- 1 cup asparagus
- 1 tsp. each of salt, pepper, and paprika

Directions

Rinse and pat dry the mahi-mahi fillets. In a bowl, whisk together the melted butter, parmesan cheese, salt, pepper, and paprika. Brush the sauce on top of the mahi-mahi and asparagus. Place the mahi-mahi and asparagus on a baking sheet or piece of aluminum foil. Place in the air fryer at 350 for 12-15 minutes and serve with rice.

Nutritional Facts: Kcal 643; Fat 16.7g; Protein 44.1g; Carbs 75.8g

Parmesan Cod

 10 Minutes

 8 Minutes

 4 Servings

Ingredients

- 4 8oz. cod fillets
- 1 cup almond flour
- 1 cup breadcrumbs
- ½ cup parmesan cheese
- ¼ cup butter
- 2 tbsp. minced garlic
- 2 sliced lemon
- 1 tsp. each of salt, pepper, and paprika

Directions

Rinse and pat dry the cod fillets. Place flour in a shallow bowl. In another bowl, combine breadcrumbs, parmesan, salt, pepper, and paprika. Dunk the cod in the flour and then the breadcrumbs. Place the cod on a baking sheet or piece of aluminum foil and add a slice of butter, a slice of lemon, and the minced garlic on top of each fillet. Fry the cod at 380 °F for 8 minutes or until the parmesan is golden brown.

Nutritional Facts: Kcal 400; Fat 21g; Protein 30.3g; Carbs 25.5g

Falafel

 5 Minutes

 15 Minutes

 4 Servings

Ingredients

- 1 can chickpeas
- 4 tbsp. flour
- ⅓ cup chopped cilant[r]
- ⅓ cup chopped parsle[y]
- 3 cloves garlic, mince[d]
- 1 chopped shallot
- 1 tsp. lemon juice
- 1 tbsp. sesame seeds
- 1 tsp. each of salt, pepper, cumin, and paprika

Directions

Rinse and drain the chickpeas. In a bowl, make a rough paste with the chickpeas, flour, cilantro, parsley, garlic, shallot, lemon juice, sesame seeds, salt, pepper, cumin, and paprika. Place a sheet of parchment in the air fryer and spray with cooking oil. Fry the falafel at 350 °F for 14 minutes, flipping halfway until the outside is golden brown and crispy.

Nutritional Facts: Kcal 231; Fat 4.3g; Protein 11.3g; Carbs 38.4g

Brussel Sprouts with Bacon

 15 Minutes

 12 Minutes

 4 Servings

Ingredients

- 1lb. Brussels sprouts
- ¼ cup chopped bacon or 4 slices
- 1 tbsp. olive oil
- 1 tbsp. maple syrup
- 1 tbsp. balsamic vinegar
- Salt and pepper to taste

Directions

Cook your bacon in the air fryer at 350 °F for 7-10 minutes. Meanwhile, rinse, trim and vertically chop the sprouts. In a large bowl, generously coat the sprouts with bacon, olive oil, maple syrup, balsamic vinegar, salt, and pepper. Place a sheet of parchment at the bottom of your air fryer and fry at 400 °F for 12 minutes, shaking them halfway.

Nutritional Facts: Kcal 196; Fat 11.8g; Protein 11g; Carbs 14g

Halloumi Cheese Burger

 10 Minutes

 10-12 Minutes

 4 Servings

Ingredients

- 1 block of Halloumi cheese
- 2 sliced avocado
- 1 cup arugula
- 1 sliced cucumber
- 1 white onion, sliced
- 4 multigrain burger buns
- 2 tbsp. olive oil
- Salt and pepper to taste

Directions

Slice the halloumi into ½-inch slices and coat with 1 tbsp of olive oil. Place the halloumi in the air fryer at 360 °F for 10-12 minutes or until the cheese begins to turn golden brown. Once the halloumi is done, assemble the burger by placing a layer of arugula, cucumber, avocado, and onion on top of the bottom bun. Then add a slice of halloumi and top with more onion and a drizzle of olive oil. Add salt and pepper to taste.

Nutritional Facts: Kcal 682; Fat 45.4g; Protein 24g; Carbs 50.4g

Cauliflower Bites

 10 Minutes

 15 Minutes

 6 Servings

Ingredients

- 3 cups cauliflower florets
- 2 large eggs
- 1 cup breadcrumbs
- 1 tsp. each of salt, pepper, paprika, garlic powder and onion powder
- ¼ cup mayonnaise
- ¼ cup greek yogurt
- ¼ cup crumbled blue cheese
- 1 tsp. hot sauce of choice

Directions

In a large bowl, mix the cauliflower, garlic powder, onion powder, salt, pepper, and paprika. In a separate bowl, whisk the eggs and pour on top of the cauliflower. When each cauliflower is coated in egg, pour the breadcrumbs into the bowl and toss. Once all of the cauliflower bites are breaded, add them to a 350 °F air fryer for 14 minutes, shaking the basket halfway. Meanwhile in a small bowl, combine the mayonnaise, Greek yogurt, blue cheese, and hot sauce and refrigerate until needed.

Nutritional Facts: Kcal 172; Fat 7.7g; Protein 7.6g; Carbs 18.6g

Fried Ravioli

 10 Minutes

 10 Minutes

 3 Servings

Ingredients

- 1 package of fresh spinach and mozzarella ravioli
- 1 large egg
- ½ cup breadcrumbs
- ¼ cup grated parmesan cheese
- 1 tsp. each of basil, oregano, thyme, salt, and pepper
- 1 cup marinara sauce

Directions

In a small bowl, whisk the egg. In a separate shallow bowl, combine the breadcrumbs, parmesan, basil, oregano, thyme, salt, and pepper. Generously coat the ravioli into the egg and then into the breadcrumbs. Place the ravioli in the air fryer at 350 °F for 10 minutes, flipping halfway. Be sure not to overlap the ravioli. Meanwhile, heat the marinara sauce and place in a dipping bowl.

Nutritional Facts: Kcal 246; Fat 7.4g; Protein 10.9g; Carbs 34.3g

Zucchini Fritters

 15 Minutes

 10 Minutes

 4 Servings

Ingredients

- 2 large zucchinis
- 1 large egg
- ½ cup flour
- ½ tsp. baking powder
- ¼ cup parmesan cheese
- 2 chopped chives
- 1 tsp. lemon juice
- 1 tsp. each of garlic powder, onion powder, and paprika
- Salt and pepper to taste

Directions

Into a bowl, grate the zucchinis and sprinkle with salt. Let sit for 10 minutes, then squeeze out any extra moisture. Add the egg, flour, baking powder, cheese, chives, lemon juice, onion powder, garlic powder, paprika, salt, and pepper. Form into about 7-8 fritters. Place the fritters on a piece of parchment in the air fryer and fry at 350 °F for 10 minutes, flipping halfway.

Nutritional Facts: Kcal 105; Fat 1.8g; Protein 5.4g; Carbs 18.4g

Zucchini Cheese Boats

Ingredients

 5 Minutes

 15 Minutes

 4 Servings

- 2 zucchinis
- 1 cup cooked rice
- ½ shredded rotisserie chicken
- 1 cup grated parmesan cheese
- 1 tsp. minced garlic
- 1 tsp. each of salt, pepper, and paprika
- 1 sprig dill
- ½ sliced cucumber

Directions

Rinse and slice the zucchini vertically. Using a spoon, scoop out the seeds and part of the flesh from the center of the zucchini. Be sure to leave enough of the flesh so that the zucchini boats won't tip over in the air fryer. In a large bowl, combine the rice, chicken, garlic, salt, pepper, and paprika. Scoop the rice mixture into the zucchini boats and top with parmesan cheese. Place in the air fryer at 400 °F for 10-15 minutes or until the cheese is fully melted and browning. Plate with the sprig of dill and a couple of slices of cucumber on each boat.

Nutritional Facts: Kcal 323; Fat 9.3g; Protein 17.7g; Carbs 43.3g

Fried Dill Pickles

Ingredients

 5 Minutes

 10-12 Minutes

 6 Servings

- 1 jar dill pickle spears
- ½ cup flour
- ½ cup buttermilk
- 1 large egg
- 1 ½ cup breadcrumbs
- 1 tsp. each of garlic powder, onion powder, salt, pepper, and paprika

Directions

Using three shallow bowls, place the flour in one bowl, the buttermilk and eggs in the second bowl, and the breadcrumbs, garlic powder, onion powder, salt, pepper, and paprika in the third bowl. Drain the pickles, rinse, and pat dry. Fully coat the pickle spears into the flour, then the buttermilk, and then the breadcrumbs. Spray the pickle spears with cooking spray and fry in the air fryer at 400 °F for 10-12 minutes, flipping halfway.

Nutritional Facts: Kcal 176; Fat 2.7g; Protein 6.8g; Carbs 30.9g

Portobello Pizzas

 5 Minutes

 10 Minutes

 4 Servings

Ingredients

- 4 portobello mushroom caps
- ½ cup marinara sauce
- ½ cup shredded mozzarella cheese
- ¼ cup olive oil
- 2 tsp. oregano
- 2 tsp. basil
- Salt and pepper to taste

Directions

Wash and pat dry the mushroom caps. Scoop the marinara sauce into the cavity of the mushroom caps and top with basil. Add a layer of mozzarella cheese, oregano, basil, salt, and pepper onto each mushroom. Place the mushroom pizzas into the air fryer at 350 °F for 10 minutes or until the cheese begins to brown.

Nutritional Facts: Kcal 155; Fat 14.2g; Protein 2.4g; Carbs 6.4g

Crumbed Asparagus

 10 Minutes

 10 Minutes

 4 Servings

Ingredients

- 1 lb. asparagus
- 2 large eggs
- ½ cup flour
- 1 cup breadcrumbs
- ⅔ cup mayonnaise
- 1 tbsp. lemon juice
- ½ tsp. minced garlic
- 1 tsp. of garlic powder, salt, and pepper

Directions

Rinse and trim the asparagus. Using three shallow bowls, place flour in the first bowl, whisk the eggs in the second bowl, and in the third bowl, combine breadcrumbs, garlic powder, salt, and pepper. Roll the asparagus in the flour, then the egg, and then the breadcrumbs. Repeat this process until all of the asparagus are fully coated. Place in the air fryer and lightly coat with cooking spray. Fry at 400 °F for 8-10 minutes. Meanwhile, in a bowl, combine the mayonnaise, lemon juice, and minced garlic to create a lemon aioli dip.

Nutritional Facts: Kcal 380; Fat 17.4g; Protein 11.4g; Carbs 46.4g

Stuffed Potatoes

 10 Minutes

 5-7 Minutes

 2 Servings

Ingredients

- 2 Yukon gold potatoes
- 1 cup baby spinach
- 1 sliced yellow bell pepper
- ¼ cup tomatoes
- ¼ cup goat cheese
- 1 sliced white radish
- ¼ cup walnuts
- 2 tbsp. olive oil
- 1 tsp. salt and pepper

Directions

Rinse and slice the potatoes a third of the way through and pull apart the slides. Season the potatoes with 1 tbsp olive oil, salt, and pepper. Place in the air fryer at 400 °F for 5-7 minutes or until the flesh is fully roasted. Remove the potato from the air fryer and let cool. Once the potato is cooled, top with the baby spinach, bell pepper, tomatoes, goat cheese, white radish, walnut, and a drizzle of olive oil.

Nutritional Facts: Kcal 405; Fat 25.2g; Protein 11g; Carbs 44.1g

Jalapeno Poppers

 10 Minutes

 8 Minutes

 4 Servings

Ingredients

- 10 jalapeños
- 1 cup shredded Mexican blend cheese
- 8 oz. cream cheese
- 2 tsp. chopped green onion
- 1 tsp. each of garlic powder, smoked paprika, salt, and pepper

Directions

Wash and cut all of the jalapeños into halves, making sure to remove all of the seeds. In a bowl, combine the cream cheese, green onion, garlic powder, salt, and pepper. Scoop about 1 tablespoon of the cream cheese mixture into each jalapeño. Top each jalapeño with cheese and paprika. Fry in the air fryer at 370 °F for 8 minutes or until the cheese begins to brown.

Nutritional Facts: Kcal 337; Fat 30g; Protein 12.1g; Carbs 5.3g

Vegetables Samosas

Ingredients

 1 Hour

 25 Minutes

 6 Servings

- 5 Yukon gold potatoes
- 1 cup sweet peas
- 1 tsp. chopped cilantro
- 2 cups flour
- 6 tbsp. vegetable oil
- 1 cup water
- 1 tsp. each of turmeric powder, chili powder, salt, and pepper

Directions

Dice the potatoes and boil for 25 minutes. Meanwhile add the flour, salt, and 3 tbsp of vegetable oil to bowl. Slowly add water while you knead the samos dough. Lightly coat the dough in vegetable oil and le sit for 20 minutes. Mash the potatoes and add to medium heat skillet. Add the salt, pepper, turmeric, chi powder, peas, and cilantro. Roll out the dough, cut 7 inch circles, and cut the circles in half. Place about tablespoons of the filling at the center. Close the edge with a pinch of water. Fry the samosas at 350 °F fc 20-25 minutes, flipping halfway.

Nutritional Facts: Kcal 402; Fat 14.4g; Protein 8.7g Carbs 61.3g

Fried Green Tomatoes Chips

Ingredients

 10 Minutes

 8 Minutes

 4 Servings

- 4 green tomatoes
- 2 large eggs
- ⅓ cup breadcrumbs
- ⅓ cup cornmeal
- ½ cup flour
- 1 tsp. each of salt, pepper, paprika, and cayenne pepper

Directions

Rinse and slice the tomatoes into ¼-inch thick discs. Sprinkle salt over the tomatoes and allow them to sit for 5 minutes. Then, using three shallow bowls, place flour in the first bowl, whisk the eggs in the second bowl, and in the third bowl, combine the breadcrumbs, cornmeal, paprika, pepper, and cayenne pepper. First, coat the tomatoes in the flour, then the egg, and then the breadcrumbs. Place in the air fryer at 400 °F for 8 minutes, flipping halfway.

Nutritional Facts: Kcal 189; Fat 3.8g; Protein 8g; Carbs 31.5g

Calamari

 10 Minutes

 8 Minutes

 4 Servings

Ingredients

- 8 oz. squid rings
- 2 cups breadcrumbs
- 1 cup flour
- 1 large egg
- ¼ cup buttermilk
- 1 lemon
- 1 tbsp. fresh parsley
- 1 tsp. each of cayenne pepper, salt, and pepper

Directions

Rinse and pat dry the squid rings. Using three shallow bowls, place flour in the first bowl, whisk the eggs and buttermilk in the second bowl, and in the third bowl, combine the breadcrumbs, cayenne pepper, salt, and pepper. Dunk the squid rings in the flour, then the egg, and then the breadcrumbs. Spray the inside of the air fryer with cooking oil and fry the squid rings at 400 °F for 6-8 minutes, flipping halfway. Plate with lemon wedges and a sprinkle of parsley.

Nutritional Facts: Kcal 411; Fat 55g; Protein 21.7g; Carbs 67.3g

Mozzarella Sticks

 35 Minutes

 8 Minutes

 8 Servings

Ingredients

- 8 mozzarella sticks
- 1 large egg
- 1 cup breadcrumbs
- ¼ cup flour
- 1 tsp. each of onion powder, garlic powder, salt, pepper, and paprika

Directions

Place the mozzarella sticks on a parchment-lined tray in the freezer for 30 minutes. Using three shallow bowls, place flour in the first bowl, whisk the eggs in the second bowl, and in the third bowl, combine the breadcrumbs, onion powder, garlic powder, salt, pepper, and paprika. Dunk the frozen mozzarella sticks in the flour, then the egg, and then the breadcrumbs. Repeat the egg and breadcrumb dip a second time if not fully coated. Place in the air fryer at 390 °F for 8 minutes or until they are golden brown.

Nutritional Facts: Kcal 158; Fat 6.4g; Protein 11g; Carbs 14g

Avocado Fries

 10 Minutes

 8 Minutes

 4 Servings

Ingredients

- 2 avocados
- ½ cup flour
- 2 large eggs
- 1 cup breadcrumbs
- 1 tsp. each of salt, pepper, and paprika
- 1 tbsp. apple cider vinegar
- 1 tbsp. Sriracha
- ¼ cup ketchup
- 2 tbsp. mayonnaise

Directions

Slice the avocados into ½-inch slices. Using three shallow bowls, place flour in the first bowl, whisk the eggs in the second bowl, and in the third bowl, combine the breadcrumbs, salt, pepper, and paprika. Dunk the avocado slices in the flour, then the egg, and then the breadcrumbs. Fry the avocado fries in the air fryer at 400 °F for 8 minutes, flipping halfway. In a small bowl, combine the apple cider vinegar, Sriracha, ketchup, and mayonnaise.

Nutritional Facts: Kcal 452; Fat 26g; Protein 10.6g; Carbs 46.5g

Mac & Cheese Snack

 30 Minutes

 10 Minutes

4 Servings

Ingredients

- 4 cups prepared macaroni and cheese
- 3 tbsp. flour
- 2 large eggs
- 1 tbsp. buttermilk
- 1 cup breadcrumbs
- 1 tsp. each of salt, pepper, and paprika
- 1 tsp. onion and garlic powder
- ½ cup ketchup
- 2 tbsp. Worcestershire sauce

Directions

Form 2-inch balls of macaroni and cheese. If the balls are not holding their form, place in the freezer for 20 minutes. Using three shallow bowls, place flour in the first bowl, whisk the eggs and buttermilk in the second bowl, and in the third bowl, combine the breadcrumbs, garlic powder, salt, pepper, and paprika. Dunk the macaroni and cheese balls in the flour, then the egg, and then the breadcrumbs. Fry the macaroni and cheese bites in the air fryer at 350 °F for 10 minutes, flipping halfway. In a small bowl, combine the ketchup, onion powder, and Worcestershire sauce.

Nutritional Facts: Kcal 411; Fat 10.3g; Protein 16.7g; Carbs 62.9g

Baked Green Beans

 10 Minutes

 8 Minutes

 4 Servings

Ingredients

- ½ lb. green beans
- ½ cup flour
- 2 large eggs
- ½ cup breadcrumbs
- ¼ cup parmesan cheese
- 1 tsp. each of garlic powder, salt, and pepper

Directions

Rinse and pat dry the green beans. Using three shallow bowls, place flour in the first bowl, whisk the eggs in the second bowl, and in the third bowl combine the breadcrumbs, parmesan, garlic powder, salt, and pepper. Coat the green beans in the flour, then the egg, and then the breadcrumbs. Fry the green beans at 400 °F for 8 minutes, tossing halfway.

Nutritional Facts: Kcal 212; Fat 6.5g; Protein 12.3g; Carbs 27.2g

Kale Chips

 10 Minutes

 5 Minutes

 4 Servings

Ingredients

- 6 oz. kale
- ¼ cup parmesan cheese
- 1 tbsp. olive oil
- 1 tsp. salt and pepper

Directions

Rinse and massage your kale in a bowl for about 5 minutes. Remove the stems from the kale and drizzle the parmesan cheese, olive oil, salt, and pepper onto the kale. Place in the air fryer at 350 °F for 5 minutes.

Nutritional Facts: Kcal 97; Fat 6.5g; Protein 5.8g; Carbs 5.3g

Pumpkin Fries

 10 Minutes

 12 Minutes

 2 Servings

Ingredients

- 1 small pumpkin
- 2 tbsp. vegetable oil
- 1 tsp. each of onion powder, garlic powder, brown sugar, cinnamon, cayenne pepper, sea salt, and pepper

Directions

Using a sharp knife, cut open the pumpkin and remove the seeds. Slice the pumpkin into 4-inch strips. In a bowl, toss the pumpkin fries with the vegetable oil, onion powder, garlic powder, brown sugar, cinnamon, cayenne pepper, sea salt, and pepper. Place in the air fryer at 400 °F for 12 minutes, flipping halfway.

Nutritional Facts: Kcal 199; Fat 14g; Protein 2.7g; Carbs 19.6g

Onion Rings and White Sauce

 10 Minutes

 10 Minutes

 5 Servings

Ingredients

- 3 large sweet onion
- 1 cup flour
- 3 large eggs
- ¾ cup buttermilk
- 2 tbsp. cornstarch
- 3 cups breadcrumbs
- ½ cup mayonnaise
- 1 tsp. parsley
- 1 tsp. garlic powder
- 1 tsp. salt, pepper, and paprika

Directions

Chop the onions into 3-inch discs and remove the center rings. Using three shallow bowls, place flour and cornstarch in the first bowl, whisk the eggs and buttermilk in the second bowl, and in the third bowl, combine the breadcrumbs, salt, pepper, and paprika. Dunk the onion rings in the flour, then the egg, and then the breadcrumbs. Fry the onion rings at 350 °F for 10 minutes, flipping halfway. In a small bowl, whisk together the mayonnaise, parsley, and garlic powder.

Nutritional Facts: Kcal 546; Fat 14.9g; Protein 17.5g; Carbs 85.1g

Sweet Potato Chips

 10 Minutes

 20 Minutes

 4 Servings

Ingredients

- 2 medium sweet potatoes
- 1 tbsp. olive oil
- 2 tsp. chili powder
- 2 tbsp. brown sugar
- 1 tsp. each of cumin, salt, and pepper

Directions

Rinse and peel the sweet potatoes and cut into ¼-inch slices. In a large bowl, toss the sweet potato slices with olive oil, chili powder, brown sugar, cumin, salt, and pepper. In a single layer, place the sweet potato slices into the air fryer at 360 °F for 20 minutes, tossing the basket halfway.

Nutritional Facts: Kcal 143; Fat 4g; Protein 1.5g; Carbs 26.6g

Crunchy Chickpeas

 5 Minutes

 15 Minutes

 4 Servings

Ingredients

- 19 oz. can of chickpeas
- 2 tbsp. olive oil
- 1 tbsp. lime juice
- 1 tsp. each of garlic powder, onion powder, cumin, salt, pepper, and paprika

Directions

Rinse and drain the chickpeas. In a large bowl, toss the chickpeas with olive oil, lime juice, garlic powder, onion powder, cumin, salt, pepper, and paprika. Fry in the air fryer at 390 °F for 12-15 minutes. Toss and spray with cooking oil halfway through.

Nutritional Facts: Kcal 231; Fat 8.7; Protein 7.1g; Carbs 32.7g

Tortilla Chips

 10 Minutes

 10 Minutes

 4 Servings

Ingredients

- 6 corn tortillas
- 1 tbsp. olive oil
- 2 tbsp. lime juice
- 1 tsp. chili powder
- 2 tomatoes
- 1 diced red onion
- 1 tbsp. chopped cilantro
- 1 tsp. salt and pepper

Directions

In a small bowl, combine the olive oil, lime juice, chili powder, and half of the salt. Brush the mixture onto both sides of the tortillas and slice the tortillas into eighths to form triangles. Place in the air fryer at 350 °F for 5 minutes. Do not overlap the tortillas in the air fryer. Meanwhile, combine the tomatoes, red onion, cilantro, salt, and pepper into a bowl.

Nutritional Facts: Kcal 141; Fat 4.8g; Protein 3g; Carbs 23.6g

Stuffed Ascolana Olives

 10 Minutes

 10 Minutes

 4 Servings

Ingredients

- 10 oz. jar of stuffed Ascolana olives
- ¾ cup flour
- 2 large eggs
- 2 cups breadcrumbs
- 1 tsp. each of garlic powder, chili powder, salt, pepper, and paprika

Directions

Drain the olives. Using three shallow bowls, place flour in the first bowl, whisk the eggs in the second bowl, and the third bowl, combine the breadcrumbs, garlic powder, chili powder, salt, pepper, and paprika. Dunk the olives in the flour, then the egg, and then the breadcrumbs. Fry the olives at 400 °F for 10 minutes, flipping halfway.

Nutritional Facts: Kcal 526; Fat 24.5g; Protein 13g; Carbs 57.8g

Cheesecake

 20 Minutes

 50 Minutes

 4 Servings

Ingredients

- 8 oz. cream cheese
- 3 tbsp. sugar
- 1 large egg
- 1 tsp. vanilla extract
- 1 ½ cup crushed graham crackers
- ¼ cup brown sugar
- 5 tbsp. melted butter
- 1 tsp. lemon juice
- 1 tsp. salt

Directions

Combine the crushed graham crackers, butter, brown sugar, and salt. Place the mixture into a parchment-lined pan with greased sides. Fry the crust in the air fryer at 300 °F for 8 minutes. Meanwhile, in a large bowl, whisk together the cream cheese, sugar, egg, and vanilla extract until slightly fluffy. Pour the cheesecake filling into the crust and place in the air fryer at 300 °F for 12 minutes. Turn the air fryer off and allow the cheesecake to sit for 30 minutes. Chill for at least 3 hours or overnight before serving.

Nutritional Facts: Kcal 548; Fat 38.6g; Protein 8.2g; Carbs 43.9g

Molten Lava Cake

 15 Minutes

 10 Minutes

 2 Servings

Ingredients

- 4 ½ tbsp. unsalted butter
- 2 large eggs
- 2 oz. bittersweet chocolate
- ¼ cup flour
- ⅓ cup granulated sugar
- ¼ tsp. salt
- ¼ cup blueberries
- 2 scoops vanilla bean ice cream
- ¼ cup chocolate syrup

Directions

Microwave the butter and chocolate in a microwave-safe bowl in 15-second intervals. In a second bowl, whisk together the eggs and sugar. Slowly fold the egg and sugar mixture into the butter and chocolate, then sift in the flour and salt. Spray ramekins with cooking oil and pour the batter into them. Place in the air fryer at 375 °F for 10 minutes. Serve with a scoop of vanilla ice cream, blueberries, and chocolate syrup.

Nutritional Facts: Kcal 804; Fat 48g; Protein 12.5g; Carbs 95.6g

Mini Apple Pies

 15 Minutes

 10 Minutes

 4 Servings

Ingredients

- 2 peeled and sliced Fuji apples
- 1 pie crust
- ¼ cup sugar.
- 2 tbsp. melted butte
- 1 tsp. cornstarch
- 2 tsp. cinnamon
- 1 tsp. nutmeg

Directions

In a bowl, combine the apples, sugar, cornstarch, cinnamon, and nutmeg. Spray a four-cup muffin tin with cooking oil and cut the pie crust into 4-inch circles. Place each pie circle into the muffin tin, coat with the melted butter, and fry at 320 °F for 5 minutes or until slightly golden brown. Add 2-3 tablespoons of the apple pie filling to the crust and fry for another 5 minutes.

Nutritional Facts: Kcal 459; Fat 21.2g; Protein 3g; Carbs 68.7g

Cannoli

 30 Minutes

 6 Minutes

 8 Servings

Ingredients

- 2 cups flour
- 1 large egg yolk
- 2 tbsp. cold butter
- 2 tsp. sugar
- 1 cup ricotta cheese
- 1 cup heavy cream
- ⅔ cup powdered sugar
- ¼ cup crushed pistachios
- 1 tsp. sea salt

Directions

In a large bowl, combine the flour, cold butter, and sugar until it forms a shaggy dough. Add the egg yolk and knead the dough on a floured work surface. Form the dough into a large sphere and place in the refrigerator for 10 minutes. Meanwhile, whisk together the ricotta, powdered sugar, and salt. In a separate bowl, whisk the heavy cream until it forms stiff peaks. Fold the whipping cream into the ricotta mixture. Remove the dough from the refrigerator and roll it out until it is ⅛-inch thick. Cut out 4-inch circles and wrap around oiled cannoli tubes. Fry at 400 °F for 6 minutes. Fill with the cannoli cream, sprinkle the pistachios on each end, and lightly dust with powdered sugar.

Nutritional Facts: Kcal 288; Fat 12.2g; Protein 7.6g; Carbs 37.2g

Chocolate Chips Cookies

 40 Minutes

 5 Minutes

 6 Servings

Ingredients

- 1 cup chocolate chips
- ½ cup melted butter
- 1 ½ cup flour
- 1 tsp. baking soda
- 1 large egg
- ½ cup brown sugar
- ¼ cup sugar
- 1 tsp. vanilla extract
- 1 tsp. salt

Directions

In a large mixing bowl, combine the melted butter, brown sugar, and white sugar. Beat in the egg and vanilla. Add the chocolate chips, baking soda, vanilla extract, and salt. Refrigerate the cookie dough for 30 minutes. Form balls of 2 tablespoons of the cookie dough, place into the parchment-lined air fryer, and cook at 350 °F for 5 minutes.

Nutritional Facts: Kcal 490; Fat 24.8g; Protein 6.6g; Carbs 60.8g

Glazed Donuts

 30 Minutes

 6 Minutes

12 Servings

Ingredients

- 3 cups flour
- ¼ cup sugar
- 1 cup milk
- 1 large egg
- ⅔ cup melted salted butter
- 2 ½ tsp. active dry yeast
- 2 cups powdered sugar
- 4 tbsp. hot water
- 2 tsp. vanilla extract

Directions

In a large bowl, combine milk, yeast, and 1 teaspoon of the sugar. Let it sit until the mixture foams. Add the rest of the sugar, 2 cups of the flour, ⅓ cup of the melted butter, and the egg. Slowly add the remaining flour while mixing until the dough doesn't stick to the sides. Allow the dough to rise until it has doubled in size. On a floured surface, roll out the dough to ½-inch thickness and cut into donuts. Allow the donuts to rise until doubled in size. Coat the air fryer with cooking spray and cook donuts at 350 °F for 6 minutes. Meanwhile, on a medium-heat skillet, add the melted butter, powdered sugar, and vanilla extract. Mix until smooth and pour over the donuts.

Nutritional Facts: Kcal 318; Fat 11.4g; Protein 4.9g; Carbs 49.4g

Strawberry Hand Cakes

 10 Minutes

 12 Minutes

 12 Servings

Ingredients

- 1 cup chopped strawberries
- 1 pie crust
- 1 large egg, whisked
- 1 tbsp. cornstarch
- 2 tbsp. sugar
- ½ tsp. vanilla extract
- 1 tbsp. lemon zest

Directions

Unroll the pie crust onto a floured work surface and roll the crust until it is ¼-inch thick. Cut 4-inch circles out of the pie crust. In a large bowl, combine the strawberries, cornstarch, sugar, vanilla extract, and lemon zest. Place 1-2 tablespoons of the strawberry filling into the center of the dough circles. Fold the dough in half and crimp the edges closed using a drop of water. Brush the egg on top of the dough. Place in the air fryer at 350 °F for 12 minutes, flipping halfway.

Nutritional Facts: Kcal 119; Fat 5.4g; Protein 1.5g; Carbs 16.7g

Brownies

 15 Minutes

 20 Minutes

 9 Servings

Ingredients

- ⅓ cup flour
- 1 cup white sugar
- 1 cup brown sugar
- 8 tbsp. salted butter
- 2 large egg
- ⅔ cup cocoa powder
- ¼ chocolate chips

Directions

Combine the butter and half of the chocolate chips into a microwave-safe bowl and microwave for 15-second intervals. Combine with the flour, white and brown sugar, eggs, and cocoa powder. Mix in the rest of the chocolate chips. Pour into a parchment-lined baking pan with the sides greased. Cook in the air fryer at 320 °F for 20 minutes. Use a toothpick to check if it is fully cooked through.

Nutritional Facts: Kcal 382; Fat 17.8g; Protein 4.6g; Carbs 56.2g

Banana Fritters

 10 Minutes

 5 Minutes

 5 Servings

Ingredients

- 4 bananas
- 2 large eggs
- 2 tbsp. milk
- ½ cup cornstarch
- ½ cup breadcrumbs
- 1 tsp. each of nutmeg, cinnamon, and cardamom
- ¼ cup powdered sugar

Directions

Peel and slice the bananas into 1-inch chunks. Using three shallow bowls, place cornstarch in the first bowl, whisk the eggs and milk in the second bowl, and in the third bowl, combine the breadcrumbs, nutmeg, cinnamon, and cardamom. Dunk the banana chunks in the cornstarch, then the egg, and then the breadcrumbs. Fry the bananas at 360 °F for 5 minutes. Sprinkle the banana fritters with powdered sugar.

Nutritional Facts: Kcal 235; Fat 3.2g; Protein 5.3g; Carbs 48.3g

Funnel Cake

 10 Minutes

 5 Minutes

 12 Servings

Ingredients

- ½ cup flour
- 1 tbsp. sugar
- 1 large egg
- ¼ cup milk
- 1 ½ tsp. baking powder
- ½ cup Greek yogurt
- ½ tsp. vanilla extract
- ½ cup powdered sugar
- Chocolate syrup and vanilla ice cream

Directions

Combine the egg, milk, Greek yogurt, and vanilla extract. In another bowl, mix the sugar, flour, and baking powder, and add the wet ingredients, mixing until a batter forms. Place into a piping bag or a sandwich bag with one tip cut off and pipe the funnel cakes into a parchment-lined air fryer. Fry the funnel cakes at 375 °F for 5 minutes or until all of the butter has turned a light brown. Top with powdered sugar, chocolate syrup, and vanilla ice cream.

Nutritional Facts: Kcal 97; Fat 1.9g; Protein 4.9g; Carbs 15.4g

Bluebbery Muffins

 10 Minutes

 14 Minutes

 8 Servings

Ingredients

- ¾ cup blueberries
- 1 cup flour
- 1 tsp. baking powder
- 1 large egg
- 3 tbsp. melted butter
- ⅓ cup milk
- 2 tbsp. sugar
- 2 tsp. vanilla extract
- ½ tsp. cinnamon

Directions

In a large bowl, combine the flour, baking powder, sugar, and cinnamon. In a separate bowl, whisk together the egg, melted butter, milk, and vanilla extract. Add the wet ingredients into the dry ingredients and mix. Add the blueberries and pour the muffin batter into silicone muffin molds. Place in the air fryer at 320 °F for 14 minutes. Use a toothpick to check that the muffins are cooked through.

Nutritional Facts: Kcal 132; Fat 5.4g; Protein 2.9g; Carbs 18g

Berry Scones

 10 Minutes

 6 Minutes

 8 Servings

Ingredients

- ¼ cup blueberries
- 1 cup flour
- 1 egg
- ¼ cup buttermilk
- 2 tbsp. butter
- ¼ cup sugar
- ½ tsp. baking powder and baking soda
- ½ tsp. vanilla extract
- 1 tbsp. orange zest

Directions

In a bowl, combine the flour, butter, sugar, baking soda, and baking powder. Slowly add the egg, buttermilk, vanilla extract, and ½ tsp of orange zest. Last, add the blueberries and mix until you get a shaggy dough. Knead the dough on a floured work surface and roll until it is ½-inch thick. Cut 1-inch circles out of the dough. Place in a parchment-lined air fryer and fry at 360 °F for 6 minutes or until the scones are golden brown. Top with the rest of the orange zest.

Nutritional Facts: Kcal 121; Fat 3.7g; Protein 2.6g; Carbs 19.5g

Apple Turnover

 15 Minutes

 15 Minutes

 6 Servings

Ingredients

- 2 Fuji apples
- 1 sheet Puff Pastry
- 1 large egg
- 2 tbsp. butter
- 2 tbsp. brown sugar
- 2 tbsp. sugar
- ¼ tsp. cinnamon
- ¼ tsp. nutmeg
- ¼ tsp. cardamom

Directions

In a medium-heat saucepan, add the diced and peeled apples, brown sugar, sugar, cinnamon, nutmeg, and cardamom. Allow the filling to reduce and thicken on the heat for about 6-8 minutes and allow to cool. On a floured work surface, lay out the pastry and cut into 4-inch circles. Place 2 tablespoons of the apple filling into the center of the pastry and crimp closed; use a bit of water to allow the pastry to stick to itself. Place in the air fryer at 350 °F for 15 minutes, flipping halfway.

Nutritional Facts: Kcal 340; Fat 20.6g; Protein 4.3g; Carbs 36.1g

Beignets

 1 Hour and 30 Minutes

 12 Minutes

 10 Servings

Ingredients

- 2 ½ cups flour
- ½ tbsp. active dry yeast
- 1 large egg and 1 egg yolk
- 6 tbsp. butter
- ½ cup buttermilk
- 6 tbsp. sugar
- 1 tsp. vanilla extract
- 1 tsp. salt
- ½ cup powdered sugar

Directions

In a small bowl, combine the yeast, buttermilk, and 1 tablespoon of the sugar. Allow to sit for five minutes or until it begins to foam. In a large bowl, combine the yeast mixture, flour, remaining sugar, and salt. In a third bowl, add the egg, yolk, 4 tablespoons of butter, and vanilla extract. Slowly add the wet ingredients into the flour mixture and mix until a smooth dough ball forms. Cover the dough and allow to rise for 1 hour or until doubled in size. Roll out the dough onto a flour work surface and cut into 2-inch balls. Let it sit for another 15 minutes. Place the beignets in the air fryer at 370 °F for 12 minutes, flipping halfway. Dust with powdered sugar.

Nutritional Facts: Kcal 247; Fat 8.4g; Protein 5.2g; Carbs 38g

Recipe
Index

Pork Chops 34

FISH AND SEAFOOD

Crab Cakes 35

Boom Boom Shrimp 35

Crusted Salmon 36

Bacon-Wrapped Scallops 36

Grilled Tuna Steak 37

Salmon Patties 37

Veracruz Style Tilapia 38

Breaded Fish Sticks 38

Land & Sea Cod Fillet 39

Shrimp Tacos 39

Shrimp Tostada 40

Salmon and Quinoa Patties 40

Garlic Butter Salmon 41

Teriyaki Salmon Skewers 41

Parmesan Cod 42

Mahi-Mahi Fillet 42

VEGETABLES

Brussels Sprouts with Bacon 43

Falafel 43

Cauliflower Bites 44

Halloumi Cheese Burger 44

Zucchini Fritters 45

Fried Ravioli 45

Fried Dill Pickles 46

Zucchini Egg Boats 46

Crumbed Asparagus 47

Portobello Pizzas 47

Jalapeño Poppers 48

Stuffed Potatoes 48

Fried Green Tomato Chips 49

Vegetable Samosas 49

SNACKS & SIDE DISHES

Mozzarella Sticks 50

Calamari 50

Mac & Cheese Snacks 51

Avocado Fries 51

Kale Chips 52

Baked Green Beans 52

Onion Rings and White Sauce 53

Pumpkin Fries 53

Crunchy Chickpeas 54

Sweet Potato Chips 54

Stuffed Ascolana Olives 55

Tortilla Chips 55

DESSERTS

Molten Lava Cake 56

Cheesecake 56

Cannoli 57

Mini Apple Pies 57

Chocolate Chip Cookies 58

Glazed Donut 58

Brownies 59

Strawberry Hand Cakes 59

Funnel Cake 60

Banana Fritters 60

Berry Scones 61

Blueberry Muffins 61

Apple Turnover 62

Beignets 62

Cooking
Charts

Weight

IMPERIAL	METRIC
1 ounce	29 g.
2 oz.	57 g.
3 oz.	85 g.
4 oz.	113 g.
5 oz.	141 g.
6 oz.	170 g.
7 oz.	202 g.
8 oz.	227 g.
1 pound	435 g.
2 lb.	870 g.
3 lb.	1360 g.

Temperature

F ° FAHRENHEIT	C° CELSIUS
100 °F	37 °C
150 °F	65 °C
200 °F	93 °C
250 °F	121 °C
300 °F	150 °F
325 °F	160 °C
350 °F	180 °C
375 °F	190 °C
400 °F	200 °C
425 °F	220 °C
450 °F	230°C
500 °F	260 °C
525 °F	274 °C
550 °F	288 °C

Volume

CUP	TBSP	TSP	ML.
1 C.	16 tbsp.	48 tsp.	237 ml.
3/4 C.	12 tbsp.	36 tsp.	177 ml.
2/3 C.	10.5 tbsp.	32 tsp.	158 ml.
1/2 C.	8 tbsp.	24 tsp.	118 ml.
1/3 C.	5.5 tbsp.	16 tsp.	79 ml.
1/4 C.	4 tbsp.	12 tsp.	59 ml.
1/6 C.	2.5 tbsp.	8 tsp.	40 ml.
1/8 C.	2 tbsp.	6 tsp.	30 ml.
1/16 C.	1 tbsp.	3 tsp.	15 ml.

Notes

Made in the USA
Coppell, TX
19 March 2022